'St Benedict ⸻ ⸻ ⸺n, nor did
he intend to ⸻ ⸻ monastic
Rule genera⸻ ⸻ to shape
Christian dis⸻ ⸻, Richard
Frost shares ⸻ ⸺late. He
offers a distill⸻ ⸻ ⸺ ⸺lp us deepen
our love of G⸻ ⸻ neighbour. Benedict sought to bring
ordinary people through the ordinary things of life closer to
the God who is everywhere. I hope those who use this book
will discover this reality for themselves and, in the words of
Benedict, "prefer nothing to the love of Christ".'

Rt Revd Robert Atwell, Bishop of Exeter

'Social scientists (such as myself) have noted with interest the
renewed attention to monasticism in late modern societies.
This fascinating book helps us to understand this. It explores
the practical as well as spiritual relevance of monastic
rhythms to daily living – in the 21st century just as any other.
I recommend it warmly.'

Grace Davie, Professor Emeritus in Sociology, University of Exeter

'A "little rule for beginners" has, by the providence of God, had
an influence far beyond the expectations of its writer. Not only
has it been the foundation of western monasticism, but it has
inspired countless readers to reflect upon the gospel way of life
as encapsulated by St Benedict. Among them is Oblate Richard
Frost, and he is to be thanked for sharing his insights with us.'

Dom Timothy Bavin OSB, Alton Abbey

'To discover the *Rule of St Benedict* is to encounter something
that is at once inspiring, supporting, reassuring, challenging.
Let this book be an introduction to the writing of a man who
will change your life.'

Esther de Waal, author of *Seeking God: The way of St Benedict*

The Bible Reading Fellowship
15 The Chambers, Vineyard
Abingdon OX14 3FE
brf.org.uk

The Bible Reading Fellowship (BRF) is a Registered Charity (233280)

ISBN 978 0 85746 813 0
First published 2019
10 9 8 7 6 5 4 3 2 1 0

Acknowledgements
Scripture quotations are from The New Revised Standard Version of the Bible,
Anglicised edition, copyright © 1989, 1995 by the Division of Christian Education of
the National Council of the Churches of Christ in the United States of America. Used
by permission. All rights reserved.

Extracts from the *Rule of St Benedict* taken from *A Reader's Version of the Rule of
Saint Benedict* in Inclusive Language © Benedictine Sisters of Erie, 1989 (updated at
eriebenedictines.org/daily-rule). Used by kind permission.

p. 198: R.S. Thomas, 'Eternity is More Than Enough' in *Collected Later Poems
1988–2000* (Bloodaxe Books, 2004). Reproduced with permission of Bloodaxe Books.
www.bloodaxebooks.com.

Every effort has been made to trace and contact copyright owners for material used
in this resource. We apologise for any inadvertent omissions or errors, and would
ask those concerned to contact us so that full acknowledgement can be made in
the future.

A catalogue record for this book is available from the British Library

Printed and bound by CPI Group (UK) Ltd, Croydon CR0 4YY

Life with St Benedict

The Rule reimagined for everyday living

Richard Frost

Thank you to Abbot Giles Hill OSB and the community at Alton Abbey for their prayers and support in my own spiritual journey. Gratitude also goes to the many people who have, knowingly and unknowingly, shared their wisdom and shown me what it is to encounter Christ. Particular appreciation goes to Mike Parsons and Olivia Warburton, commissioning editors at BRF, whose enthusiasm and advice has enabled this book to be held in your hands. And, of course, very special thanks to Jane, my wife, and Jonathan and Rachel for their loving companionship on this journey of life.

Contents

Foreword

Outside the common room and within the cloister of Alton Abbey, there is, on the wall, an oak carving of St Benedict. In his right hand he is holding a flaming torch with the word '*pax*' (peace) carved into the handle. In his left hand he is holding a book entitled '*Sancta Regula*' (holy rule), his inspired and prayer-filled writing, from living both in solitude and in community, for those who want to take a closer walk with Christ Jesus.[1]

Joan Chittister OSB points out that the word 'Regula', which we translate as 'rule':

> … in the ancient sense meant 'guidepost' or 'railing', something to hang on to in the dark, something that leads in a given direction, something that points out the road, something that gives us support as we climb… The Rule of Benedict is a way of life.
>
> Joan Chittister, *Wisdom Distilled from the Daily: Living the Rule of St Benedict today* (HarperCollins, 1990), p. 7

Richard Frost has given us in this book, *Life with St Benedict*, a practical presentation of that carving on the cloister wall of Alton Abbey. It offers both light, as symbolised by the torch, and a guide to using the *Rule* in the spirit that was always intended by St Benedict: accessible, understandable and a means of formation to grow closer to Christ and one's neighbour.

Our present culture has lost touch with its Christian heritage and it seems that almost anything and everything is filling that void as people seek meaning and direction. Culture terms it 'spirituality'. Richard has given us a book to be used – and if it is used according to the author's directions it will indeed give substance once again to this word 'spiritual', for it will open up for us ways to penetrate scripture, especially the prayerfulness of the Psalms and life of Jesus through the gospels. Following the *Rule of St Benedict* day by day with the gentle, experienced exercises and guidance of Richard, is to open ourselves to the promptings of the true Spirit, the Holy Spirit, the Spirit of Christ, and not the spirit of the age.

Richard has shown us in a fresh and inspirational way that a text which has stood the test of time over 1,500 years has something new to say to us. He has bestowed on us a great blessing in this work, and I am sure that for many ordinary people who wish to grow in holiness and humility this book will be invaluable for that journey.

Revd Graham Reeves OblOSB, MA Bth (Hons)

Introduction

For many people, the word 'rule' brings back memories of school life or 'breaking the rules'. Rules may have governed or influenced how a job was done or what we could and couldn't do where we lived. They apply in sport and in games, where the rules explain how to play (or make it seem far too complicated).

Then there are 'unwritten rules' and those that surround social interaction and relationships. And there are times and places where rules are followed but no one quite knows why.

Rule can also mean having dominion over people or a place. Variants to the norm are sometimes described as 'the exception to the rule'. A rule is also a twelve-inch piece of wood… not sure there's any theological significance in that, but sometimes rules do measure what we do.

Rules are paradoxical when negative commands, such as 'Don't do that', also keep us safe and healthy. The ten commandments could be described as rules aimed at enabling us to be at one with God. Christ himself gave us a new rule: 'Love one another. Just as I have loved you, you also should love one another' (John 13:34).

Rule of St Benedict

Born c. 480 AD in Nursia (present-day Norcia) in Umbria, central Italy, St Benedict is generally acknowledged to be the founder of western monasticism. Following on from the early desert fathers (such as Augustine of Hippo, John Chrysostom and John Cassian) and mothers (such as Syncletica of Alexandria, Theodora of Alexandria and Sarah of the Desert), St Benedict was the forerunner of other influential leaders, such as Bernard of Clairvaux, Bridget of Sweden, Columba (of Iona and elsewhere), Clare and Francis (of Assisi) and Dominic (founder of the Dominican Order).

St Benedict founded several monasteries, most notably at Monte Cassino, where, in the years preceding his death in 540AD, he wrote a *Rule for Monks* to guide life in a community. Drawn partly from earlier writings, what became called the *Rule of St Benedict* covers spiritual and practical aspects of living in community and became the established norm for monastic living in Europe.

Rooted in the Bible, the *Rule* is still used today to provide wisdom and guidance for nuns and monks living in monastic communities and also for individuals who have adopted a similar approach to faith and daily living, such as oblates.

From the medieval Latin *oblātus* (meaning 'to offer'), oblates can be lay or ordained, single or married, widowed or divorced, gay or straight, and are affiliated to a specific monastic community. They follow a personal 'Rule of Life' which absorbs elements of the *Rule of St Benedict* and it can provide a framework for daily prayer, reading (both biblical and other study), church attendance, giving, reflection, retreat, affiliation to a specific Benedictine community and personal commitment to family, work and relationships (there's an example of a personal Rule of Life on page 199).

Vows of St Benedict

For Benedictine nuns and monks, stability, *conversatio morum* and obedience have particular significance and meaning, and the principles of these monastic vows can be helpful for everyone.

- *Stability* for the nun and the monk is about remaining in a specific community for life. For those living outside such settings, stability often finds itself dependent on many things, such as our house, our job, our finances, the place we live, the people we know or the church we go to. And when those things happen be threatened, such as by change or uncertainty, life can feel unstable. For all seeking a deeper relationship with God, stability is found by becoming increasingly rooted in the one with whom that relationship is sought.

- *Conversatio morum* means 'fidelity to the monastic life'. However, another term has also come into use, *conversio morum* or 'conversion of life'. Under the guidance of the Holy Spirit, this conversion, or change, is necessary for our relationship with God to grow. As Bishop Richard Moth puts it, 'Conversion is a journey in which we are engaged every day of our lives, even at every moment.'[2]

- *Obedience* to the abbot or abbess is a requisite for those in monastic life but isn't solely about doing what one's told. Pope Francis describes the meaning very clearly: 'The word "obey" comes from Latin, it means to listen, to hear others. Obeying God is listening to God, having an open heart to follow the path that God points out to us. Obedience to God is listening to God and it sets us free.'[3]

For those not called to the monastic life, the principles of the vows can be seen as threads running through our faith. As we listen to God, we become increasingly aware that in order to change, stability is needed; and in order to be stable, we are also to change.

Life with St Benedict

This book is not a commentary on the *Rule of St Benedict*, nor will it explore the detail of monastic life. Many people have explored those deeper aspects much more effectively than this current writer can or aims to do (take a look at the further reading on page 201).

Here are some notes on how you may like to use this book:

- *Everyday reflections*. Benedictine communities and oblates use a well-established scheme of daily readings to enable the entire *Rule of St Benedict* to be considered over a four-month period – thus doing so three times in every year. *Life with St Benedict* follows those daily readings and by using this pattern you will be joining with thousands of others in reflecting on the *Rule* and what God may be saying on each particular day. You can start at any time and reread in the future to aid ongoing reflection.

  For each reading, there is a short reflection, which aims to help relate the words of the *Rule* and the threads of the Benedictine vows to the practicalities of modern day-to-day faith, work and life. On some days, the reflection will focus on the whole reading from the *Rule* and on other occasions, on just a sentence or two.

  How you use the readings from the *Rule* or the reflection is up to you. Don't worry if you miss a few days and, of course, there will be times when what you read will have no particular impact. Neither is it essential to read every single word – indeed, it may be that God will draw your attention to a specific phrase: in which case, dwell on that and listen to what is being said. You don't have to follow the daily pattern, but it's probably best not to read several days at once. Take your time. God's got all the time in the world for you.

  You may find it handy to have a notebook or a file on your computer or phone in which to make notes as a reminder for future rereadings. Each reflection will finish with a simple prayer.

- *The Psalms* reflect the full range of both our human emotions and our relationship with God and are an integral part of both the *Rule* and the life of Benedictine communities. The *Rule* indicates that communities are to say or sing all 150 psalms in one week, every week. That is a significant task for any community, let alone anyone else! In this book, readings from the Psalms are indicated for each day in a simple, numerical order, thus enabling you to read every psalm over a four-month period.[4] On most days, there is no deliberate link made with the rest of the entry, thus leaving the Holy Spirit to connect them with your own journey of faith. You may find it helpful to say the psalms out loud, perhaps including a doxology at the end.

- *The language.* Written 1,500 years ago, the *Rule of St Benedict* contains language, particularly in relation to punishments and the treatment of children, which sits uneasily with our 21st-century consciences, so do bear in mind the cultural differences that exist. Many translations of the *Rule* have emerged, and the one used for this book is an inclusive-language version,[5] which strives to enable the text to be related to by all. The quotations from the Bible given in the *Rule* are not always verbatim[6] and, together with some explanatory footnotes, the glossary (on p. 14) also explains some unfamiliar words or terms.

Life with St Benedict is written with ordinary, everyday Christians in mind. Whether monastic or oblate or neither, the *Rule of St Benedict* has much to say to all of us in our faith, work and daily living. The *Rule* retains a relevance to our lives in a world where change is often feared, stability can be elusive and busyness interferes with listening to God. With the grace of our Lord Jesus Christ and the wisdom of the Holy Spirit, may there be those occasions when God speaks in a way that relates to your life at this time.

Glossary

Abbot/Abbess – From Aramaic *abba* (father), the head of a community of monks/nuns. The version of the *Rule of St Benedict* used for this book uses terms such as 'abbot' and 'prioress' as a general way of naming the superior of a monastic community, whether that community is male, female or combined. Some communities will have both an abbess and a prioress (or an abbot and a prior). Nothing is to be inferred regarding gender superiority by the way these terms are used in the version of the *Rule* being quoted.

Ambrosian hymn – Hymns attributed to Aurelius Ambrosius (AD340–97), archbishop of Milan.

Cellarer – The member of a monastic community responsible for provisions such as food and drink.

Cenobite – From the Greek for 'common' and 'life', a cenobite is a member of a monastic community.

Doxology – Words traditionally said at the end of a psalm, such as: 'Glory to the Father and to the Son and to the Holy Spirit; as it was in the beginning is now and shall be for ever. Amen.'

Gyrovague – From late Latin *gyrovagus* (*gyro* – circle; *vagus* – wandering), an itinerant monk without fixed residence or leadership, who relied on charity and the hospitality of others.

Monastic – Relates to nuns, monks or others living under religious vows, or the buildings in which they live (e.g. monastic community such as an abbey, monastery, priory or convent).

Monk – From Old English *munuc*, from Greek *monakhos* (alone, solitary).

Nun – From Old English *nonne*, from Latin *nonna*, feminine of *nonnus* (monk).

Oblate – A lay or ordained person formally associated to a particular monastic community. Entitled to use the letters OblOSB or similar after their name.

Opus Dei – The 'Work of God' (also referred to as the 'Divine Office' or 'Liturgy of the Hours' or 'The Breviary'). A term used to describe the times of prayer in a monastic community and referred to in the *Rule of St Benedict* (times are approximate):

- Vigils – said in the dark in the middle of the night
- Lauds – morning prayer at dawn
- Prime – early morning prayers (first hour – 6.00 am)
- Terce – mid-morning prayers (third hour – 9.00 am)
- Sext – midday prayers (sixth hour – noon)
- None – mid-afternoon prayers (ninth hour – 3.00 pm)
- Vespers – evening prayer (6.00 pm)
- Compline – night prayer followed by complete silence (9.00 pm).

Monastic communities vary in the number, observance and the exact timing of the offices.

Oratory – From Latin *orare* (a place of prayer), the part of the monastic community building set aside solely for prayer.

OSB – Initials used after the name of a nun or monk in the Order of St Benedict. The Order of St Benedict is the name given to a confederation of autonomous monastic communities.

Prior/Prioress – From the Latin for 'earlier, first', an ecclesiastical title for a superior, usually lower in rank than an abbot or abbess. See also **Abbot/Abbess** above.

Sarabaite – A class of ascetics in the early church who lived either in their own homes or in small groups near the cities and acknowledged no monastic superior. The term is still used to describe those who follow their own religious ideas independently of ecclesiastical authority.

Senpectae – Wise and mature members of a monastic community who reach out to support, comfort and encourage wayward monks or nuns.

The prophet – St Benedict uses this title for the writer of the Psalms and, in his time, this was probably considered to be King David. The psalter was also regarded as a prophetic book.

Versicle – A short sentence or verse said or sung by the person leading the office, to which the congregation gives a response.

Everyday reflections

1 Jan, 2 May, 1 Sep

Prologue

Listen carefully, my child, to my instructions, and attend to them with the ear of your heart. This is advice from one who loves you; welcome it, and faithfully put it into practice. The labour of obedience will bring you back to God from whom you had drifted through the sloth of disobedience. This message of mine is for you, then, if you are ready to give up your own will, once and for all, and armed with the strong and noble weapons of obedience to do battle for Jesus, the Christ.

First of all, every time you begin a good work, you must pray to God most earnestly to bring it to perfection. In God's goodness, we are already counted as God's own, and therefore we should never grieve the Holy One by our evil actions. With the good gifts which are in us, we must obey God at all times that God may never become the angry parent who disinherits us, nor the dreaded one, enraged by our sins, who punishes us forever as worthless servants for refusing to follow the way to glory.

Reflection

Take ten minutes to sit with this book.
Try to be still.
Listen carefully.
What do you hear?
The noise of traffic. Children. Birds. The wind.
The constant chattering of persistent thoughts.
Things you've forgotten.

Reminders of love and loss.
Attend to those distractions with the ear of your mind.
Be still.
Listen.

As you begin your exploration of life with St Benedict, pray that God will bring it to perfection. You are already one of God's own. You already have good gifts within you.

Listen now with the ear of your heart: that which is central to your very being, that which gives your attention to God. What do you hear?

Read
Psalms 1—2

Pray
Dear God, please help me to listen.

·····†·····

2 Jan, 3 May, 2 Sep

Prologue

Let us get up then, at long last, for the scriptures rouse us when they say: 'It is high time for us to arise from sleep' (Romans 13:11). Let us open our eyes to the light that comes from God, and our ears to the voice from the heavens that every day calls out this charge: 'If you hear God's voice today, do not harden your hearts' (Psalm 95:8). And again: 'You that have ears to hear, listen to what the Spirit says to the churches' (Revelation 2:7). And what does the Spirit say? 'Come and listen to me; I will teach you to reverence God'

(Psalm 34:11). 'Run while you have the light of life, that the darkness of death may not overtake you' (John 12:35).

Reflection

Yesterday provided a starting point for stillness and listening. Now we are to fully open our eyes, our ears and our heart to live the life that God wants us to.

As we will see in a few days, St Benedict describes the *Rule* as guiding those attending 'a school for God's service'. So, in this freshers' week, the Prologue sets out some foundation-level lessons. Like all educational experiences, some of these lessons will be challenging and others affirming – but all are firmly rooted in scripture and God's desire for the very best for you.

In one sense, it doesn't matter whether our learning style is influenced by approaches such as 'the scripture moveth us, in sundry places'[7] or the expression of gifts in the charismatic. Whatever church background and faith journey thus far, consider your response to the exhortation to be awake and alert, to see God in everything and everyone, and to listen to what the Holy Spirit is saying.

You may like to think about what you can do to help you learn, for example:

- A notebook in which to record your reflections
- A candle to aid meditation
- A symbol or icon to focus upon
- Music to listen to
- A place to walk
- A specific place to sit, free from distraction.

What do you think you would like to learn most?

Read
Psalms 3—4

Pray
Dear God, please help me to learn.

·····✝·····

3 Jan, 4 May, 3 Sep

Prologue

Seeking workers in a multitude of people, God calls out and says again: 'Is there anyone here who yearns for life and desires to see good days' (Psalm 34:12)? If you hear this and your answer is 'I do,' God then directs these words to you: If you desire true and eternal life, 'keep your tongue free from vicious talk and your lips from all deceit; turn away from evil and do good; let peace be your quest and aim' (Psalm 34:13–14). Once you have done this, my eyes will be upon you and my ears will listen for your prayers; and even before you ask me, I will say to you: 'Here I am' (Isaiah 58:9). What is more delightful than this voice of the Holy One calling to us? See how God's love shows us the way of life. Clothed then with faith and the performance of good works, let us set out on this way, with the gospel for our guide, that we may deserve to see the Holy One 'who has called us to the eternal presence' (1 Thessalonians 2:12).

Reflection

Rowan Williams writes, 'If it is God's will to bring something about, some act of healing or reconciliation, some change for the better...

he has chosen that your prayer is going to be part of a set of causes that makes it happen.'[8]

Much as we may like it to be the case at times, God chooses not to do everything by himself. The remarkable thing, though, is that he asks us to be part of making it happen. God's love for us shows us the way we are to be living. Yes, there are tough standards to live by and, guided by the gospel, our faith is also to be marked by good works. But as we yearn for the fullness of life for others and ourselves and for good days on this earth, our reward is to be eternally in the presence of God.

No wonder St Benedict writes, 'What is more delightful than this voice of the Holy One calling to us?'

How does it feel to be considered part of God's work?

Read
Psalms 5—6

Pray
May I always be listening to your calling for me.

4 Jan, 5 May, 4 Sep

Prologue

If we wish to dwell in God's tent, we will never arrive unless we run there by doing good deeds. But let us ask with the prophet: 'Who will dwell in your tent, O God? who will find rest upon your holy mountain?' (Psalm 15:1). After this question, then, let us listen well to what God says in reply,

for we are shown the way to God's tent. 'Those who walk without blemish and are just in all dealings; who speak truth from the heart and have not practiced deceit; who have not wronged another in any way, not listened to slanders against a neighbour' (Psalm 15:2–3). They have foiled the evil one at every turn, flinging both the devil and these wicked promptings far from sight. While these temptations were still 'young, the just caught hold of them and dashed them against Christ' (Psalms 15:4; 137:9). These people reverence God, and do not become elated over their good deeds; they judge it is God's strength, not their own, that brings about the good in them. 'They praise' (Psalm 15:4) the Holy One working in them, and say with the prophet: 'Not to us, O God, not to us give the glory, but to your name alone' (Psalm 115:1).

Reflection

The 'tent of the Lord's presence' is an ancient sign of God being with his people. St Benedict's insight into the human condition is clear when considering the ways in which we are to dwell within it:

- Outward: Behave and speak well, for these demonstrate our faith to other people – and there is room in God's tent;

- Inward: Deal with problems at an early stage, as not doing so nearly always leads to increased difficulties. Place them firmly under Christ – and there is room in God's tent;

- Godward: Acknowledge God in all things, giving him (not ourselves) the glory – and there is room in God's tent.

How are you doing outwardly, inwardly and Godwardly?

Read
Psalms 7—8

Pray
Where possible, Lord, may all I do be to your glory.

5 Jan, 6 May, 5 Sep

Prologue

> In just this way Paul the apostle refused to take credit for the power of his preaching. He declared: 'By God's grace I am what I am' (1 Corinthians 15:10). And again, Paul said: 'They who boast should make their boast in God' (2 Corinthians 10:17). That is why it is said in the gospel: 'Whoever hears these words of mine and does them is like a wise person who built a house upon rock; the floods came and the winds blew and beat against the house, but it did not fall: it was founded on rock' (Matthew 7:24–25).

> With this conclusion, God waits for us daily to translate into action, as we should, these holy teachings. Therefore, our life span has been lengthened by way of a truce, that we may amend our misdeeds. As the apostle says: 'Do you not know that the patience of God is leading you to repent?' (Romans 2:4). And indeed, God assures us in love: 'I do not wish the death of sinners, but that they turn back to me and live' (Ezekiel 33:11).

Reflection

Oscar Wilde is reputed to have said, 'Be yourself; everyone else is already taken.'[9] Building on what was considered yesterday, stability occurs when we build our faith firmly on the rock of Christ and translate it into conversion of life. That takes time.

David Foster OSB writes, 'Conversion is a matter of letting the whole of us slowly turn towards God,'[10] a point developed by Abbot Giles Hill OSB: 'We can only be ourselves when we allow God to transform our lives. We need to be free of those things which stop us.'[11]

It is one of the great joys of God's love for us that through his grace each of us can draw closer and closer to a point of being able to say, 'I am who I am' – accepting the person I am and accepting that God's love is for the person as I am.

Read
Psalms 9—10

Pray
Help me be the person you want me to be: the person I am.

6 Jan, 7 May, 6 Sep

Prologue

Now that we have asked God, who will dwell in his holy tent, we have heard the instruction for dwelling in it, but only if we fulfil the obligations of those who live there. We must prepare our hearts and bodies for the battle of holy obedience to God's instructions. What is not possible to us by nature, let us ask the Holy One to supply by the help of grace. If we wish to reach eternal life, even as we avoid the torments of hell, then – while there is still time, while we are in this body and

have time to accomplish all these things by the light of life – we must run and do now what will profit us forever.

Reflection

St Benedict's summary of the main points of these first few days of living with the *Rule* provides a good point at which to pause.

Joan Chittister OSB writes, 'We are not capable of what we are about to do but we are not doing it alone and we are not doing it without purpose. God is with us, holding us up so that the reign of God may be made plain to us and become hope to others.'[12]

We have asked God, who will dwell in his holy tent.

'You,' he says. 'Come in.'

Read
Psalms 11—12

Pray
Thank you, Lord, for inviting me in.

7 Jan, 8 May, 7 Sep

Prologue

Therefore, we intend to establish a school for God's service. In drawing up its regulations, we hope to set down nothing harsh, nothing burdensome. The good of all concerned, however, may prompt us to a little strictness in order to

amend faults and to safeguard love. Do not be daunted immediately by fear and run away from the road that leads to salvation. It is bound to be narrow at the outset. But as we progress in this way of life and in faith, we shall run on the path of God's commandments, our hearts overflowing with the inexpressible delight of love. Never swerving from God's instructions, then, but faithfully observing God's teaching in the monastery until death, we shall through patience share in the sufferings of Christ that we may deserve also to share in the eternal presence. Amen.

Reflection

So, you've reached the end of freshers' week at the School for God's Service. There may have been times of encouragement and times when it all feels a bit too much – but that's no different from starting anything new. Give yourself time. These 'rules' are here for our benefit as we walk the way of life and faith, run with God's teaching and find our hearts overflowing with love as we come towards that time when we will share in the Lord's everlasting presence.

As you look back on this first week's teaching, what have been the main learning points for you?

Read
Psalms 13—14

Pray
Help me to learn even more, Lord.

8 Jan, 9 May, 8 Sep

Chapter 1: The kinds of monastics

There are clearly four kinds of monastics. First, there are the cenobites, that is to say, those who belong to a monastery, where they serve under a Rule and an abbot or prioress.

Second, there are the anchorites or hermits, who have come through the test of living in a monastery for a long time, and have passed beyond the first fervour of monastic life. Thanks to the help and guidance of many, they are now trained to fight against evil. They have built up their strength and go from the battle line in the ranks of their members to the single combat of the desert. Self-reliant now, without the support of another, they are ready with God's help to grapple single-handed with the vices of body and mind.

Third, there are sarabaites, the most detestable kind of monastics, who with no experience to guide them, no rule to try them as 'gold is tried in a furnace' (Proverbs 27:21), have a character as soft as lead. Still loyal to the world by their actions, they clearly lie to God by their signs of religion. Two or three together, or even alone, without a shepherd, they pen themselves up in their own sheepfolds, not God's. Their law is what they like to do, whatever strikes their fancy. Anything they believe in and choose, they call holy; anything they dislike, they consider forbidden.

Fourth and finally, there are the monastics called gyrovagues, who spend their entire lives drifting from region to region, staying as guests for three or four days in different monasteries. Always on the move, they never settle down, and are slaves to their own wills and gross appetites. In every way they are worse than sarabaites.

It is better to keep silent than to speak of all these and their disgraceful way of life. Let us pass them by, then, and with the help of God, proceed to draw up a plan for the strong kind, the cenobites.

Reflection

There are modern-day parallels with St Benedict's descriptions of sixth-century monks. We might view gyrovagues as people on a perpetual journey of disappointment in the quest for the perfect church. There are sarabaites: the 'power brokers' and the cliques in our congregations or those who 'do their own thing' without the church's agreement.

More positively, we recall people such as Julian of Norwich, an anchorite, who led lives of solitude yet engaged with the world around them. Hermits and anchorites were the pioneers of philanthropic works which in these days are undertaken and carried out by charities and public-sector organisations.[13] Some still live this way of life today.

St Benedict encourages his monks to be cenobites – simply put, to be a member of a community. The word 'cenobite' stems from the Greek for 'common' and 'life'. We are to live as believers in community. For most Christians, that community will be one which is dispersed through individual churches, but we also possess a conscious awareness that 'we who are many are one body' (1 Corinthians 10:17).

Just think that, right now, all around the world, as you read this, others will be praying, worshipping and giving God the glory – sharing the common life of faith in Christ.

Read
Psalms 15—16

Pray
Thank you, Lord, that I share this journey with others.

9 Jan, 10 May, 9 Sep

Chapter 2: Qualities of the abbot or prioress

> To be worthy of the task of governing a monastery, the prioress or abbot must always remember what the title signifies and act accordingly. They are believed to hold the place of Christ in the monastery. Therefore, a prioress or abbot must never teach or decree or command anything that would deviate from God's instructions. On the contrary, everything they teach and command should, like the leaven of divine justice, permeate the minds of the community.

Reflection

The position and responsibility of those in leadership is a theme to which the *Rule* returns frequently. Over the next few days, different aspects of leadership in our churches, workplaces and elsewhere will be explored and reflected upon.

Today, we observe two important principles. Firstly, those in leadership are deemed to be as Christ to those they lead. Secondly, those in leadership are not only to teach in line with God's instructions but are also to be distinctly mindful of the influence they have upon those they lead.

If you are in a leadership position (in church, at work or elsewhere), in what ways are you able to demonstrate those Christlike qualities?

In those situations where you are being led, consider how you might support and pray for those who are your leaders.

Read
Psalm 17

Pray
Help me to be mindful of the demands and responsibilities carried by those in leadership.

······†······

10 Jan, 11 May, 10 Sep

Chapter 2: Qualities of the abbot or prioress

Let the prioress and abbot always remember that at the judgment of God, not only their teaching but also the community's obedience will come under scrutiny. The prioress and abbot must, therefore, be aware that the shepherd will bear the blame wherever the owner of the household finds that the sheep have yielded no profit. Still, if they have faithfully shepherded a restive and disobedient flock, always striving to cure their unhealthy ways, it will be otherwise: the shepherd will be acquitted at God's judgment. Then, like the prophet, they may say to God: 'I have not hidden your justice in my heart; I have proclaimed your truth and your salvation' (Psalm 40:10) but they spurned and rejected me (Isaiah 1:2; Ezekiel 20:27). Then at last the sheep that have rebelled against their care will be punished by the overwhelming power of death.

Reflection

The role of our leaders (in church, work or elsewhere) is in some respects like that of a shepherd, and that also leads us to reflect on what type of shepherd do we tend to expect.

In the Middle East, generally speaking, shepherds go in front of the flock and the sheep follow. Each shepherd has a particular sound they make and the sheep recognise and respond to that call. In the west, the tendency is for the shepherd to drive the sheep and they may also have one or two dogs to help.

We need both types of shepherd. We need people who will lead: those who bring ideas and a vision of where we are going. And we also need people who will lead from behind, encouraging us to move forwards. And yes, we need a dog or two – people who will keep us together.

Pray for the shepherds – and the dogs – in your church, workplace or elsewhere.

Read
Psalm 18:1–30

Pray
Give wisdom to those who are our shepherds.

11 Jan, 12 May, 11 Sep

Chapter 2: Qualities of the abbot or prioress

Furthermore, those who receive the name of prioress or abbot are to lead the community by a twofold teaching: they must point out to the monastics all that is good and holy more by example than by words, proposing God's commandments to a receptive community with words, but demonstrating God's instructions to the stubborn and the dull by a living example. Again, if they teach the community that something is not to be done, then neither must they do it, 'lest after preaching to others, they themselves be found reprobate' (1 Corinthians 9:27) and God some day call to them in their sin: 'How is it that you repeat my just commands and mouth my covenant when you hate discipline and toss my words behind you' (Psalm 50:16–17)? And also, this: 'How is it that you can see a splinter in another's eye, and never notice the plank in your own' (Matthew 7:3)?

Reflection

Leading by example is both important and very influential. If a leader demonstrates good qualities – such as clear communication (in both speaking and listening) and taking time to consult about change or explaining decisions – then others will respect them, collaborate and maybe even imitate. On the other hand, those regarded as not leading by example – not doing what they say they will, not making decisions or showing signs of hypocrisy – will soon find their authority and respect are undermined. Either way, if the leader does it, the people may well do also.

In what ways can this be a reason for celebration or a cause for concern?

Read
Psalm 18:31–51

Pray
May those who are our leaders lead by example.

······✝······

12 Jan, 13 May, 12 Sep

Chapter 2: Qualities of the abbot or prioress

The prioress or abbot should avoid all favouritism in the monastery. They are not to love one more than another unless they find someone better in good works and obedience. One born free is not to be given higher rank than one born a slave who becomes a monastic, except for some other good reason. But the prioress and abbot are free, if they see fit, to change anyone's rank as justice demands. Ordinarily, all are to keep to their regular places, because 'whether slave or free, we are all one in Christ' (Galatians 3:28; Ephesians 6:8) and share equally in the service of the one God, for 'God shows no partiality among persons' (Romans 2:11). Only in this are we distinguished in God's sight: if we are found better than others in good works and in humility. Therefore, the prioress and abbot are to show equal love to everyone and apply the same discipline to all according to their merits.

Reflection

We all have our favourites: people we are attracted to, people we get on well with, people we prioritise, people we prefer to be with more than others. There will be people we admire, people who 'do good works', people who are humble, people who show love and kindness to others despite their own circumstances.

Similarly, we all know people we don't like: people who have hurt us, people whom we find difficult to talk to or be with, people we rank lower (or higher) than others.

It's challenging, isn't it – to show equal love to everyone, to love those we do not like?

Think about someone you don't like or find difficult to be with. Pray for them.

Read
Psalms 19—20

Pray
Forgive my lack of love, Lord. Help me to have greater tolerance and patience.

·····†·····

13 Jan, 14 May, 13 Sep

Chapter 2: Qualities of the abbot or prioress

In their teachings, the prioress or abbot should always observe the apostle's recommendation in which it is said: 'Use argument, appeal, reproof' (2 Timothy 4:2). This means that they must vary with circumstances, threatening and coaxing by turns, at times stern, at times devoted and tender. With the undisciplined and restless, they will use firm argument: with the obedient and docile and patient, they will appeal for greater virtue; but as for the negligent and disdainful, we charge the abbot or prioress to use reproof and rebuke. They should not gloss over the sins of those who err, but cut them out while they can, as soon as they begin to sprout, remembering the fate of Eli, priest of Shiloh (1 Samuel 2:11–4:18). For the upright and perceptive, the first and second warnings should be verbal; but those who are evil or stubborn, arrogant or disobedient, can be curbed only by blows or some other physical punishment at the first offence. It is written, 'The fool cannot be corrected with words' (Proverbs 29:19): and again, 'Strike your children with a rod and you will free their souls from death' (Proverbs 23:14).

Reflection

Whether it is standing outside the headteacher's office at school, being in front of a disciplinary hearing at work or being challenged by the police on the street, being admonished by another can be a humiliating, chastening and salutary experience.

The person meting out such justice has a huge responsibility. They are to ensure it 'varies with circumstances' – that the punishment fits the crime. St Benedict also seems to advocate a 'good cop, bad cop' approach: 'threatening and coaxing by turns, at times stern, at times devoted and tender'. In other words, to discipline with love.

We are not to ignore wrongdoing but to talk about the situation at an early stage. Indeed, not talking early is the reason why most disputes get out of hand and cause so much damage.

Read Jesus' teaching in Matthew 18:15–20.

Read
Psalm 21

Pray
May I be loving and wise in my criticism of other people.

14 Jan, 15 May, 14 Sep

Chapter 2: Qualities of the abbot or prioress

The prioress and abbot must always remember what they are and remember what they are called, aware that more will be expected of one to whom more has been entrusted. They must know what a difficult and demanding burden they have undertaken: directing souls and serving a variety of temperaments, coaxing, reproving and encouraging them as appropriate. They must so accommodate and adapt themselves to each one's character and intelligence that they will not only keep the flock entrusted to their care from dwindling, but will rejoice in the increase of a good flock.

Reflection

'While it [is] necessary to have vision, passion, make firm and decisive decisions and ensure [others do] not suffer,' writes human resources specialist Janet Arthur, 'it is equally important for a leader to demonstrate nurture and care for their people so they remain motivated and willingly come along with [them]… Different leadership approaches may be suited to different people and issues… Leadership has to have a purpose; and a key part of the leader's role is to work out which approach will best enable them to drive positive change.'[14]

Whenever there is a change in leadership, be it the church minister or the line manager, people feel less secure. 'What's the new person going to be like?' 'I don't want them to change anything.' 'If I don't like them, I'm going to leave.'

Leaders who can adapt themselves to those whom they lead and care for will build up trust and confidence. The role of a leader is key to stability. In what ways do your leaders create stability?

Read
Psalm 22

Pray
Lord, please help those who lead to be able to adapt to the hopes and the demands of those around them.

15 Jan, 16 May, 15 Sep

Chapter 2: Qualities of the abbot or prioress

Above all, they must not show too great a concern for the fleeting and temporal things of this world; neglecting or treating lightly the welfare of those entrusted to them. Rather, they should keep in mind that they have undertaken the care of souls for whom they must give an account. That they may not plead lack of resources as an excuse, they are to remember what is written: 'Seek first the reign and justice of God, and all these things will be given you as well' (Matthew 6:33) and again, 'Those who reverence the Holy One lack nothing' (Psalm 34:10).

The prioress and abbot must know that anyone undertaking the charge of souls must be ready to account for them. Whatever the number of members they have in their care, let them realize that on judgment day they will surely have to submit a reckoning to God for all their souls – and indeed for their own as well. In this way, while always fearful of the future examination of the shepherd about the sheep entrusted to them and careful about the state of others' accounts, they become concerned also about their own, and while helping others to amend by their warnings, they achieve the amendment of their own faults.

Reflection

'Doing more with less' is a commonplace expression in our society today. Public services in the UK, such as the NHS and local councils, are under great strain. Many churches, particularly in rural areas (but not exclusively so), are seeing their congregations age and dwindle. Yet we continue to see examples where those who have less are doing more because of learnt resourcefulness and reassessed priorities. Leaders have a crucial role in such situations.

'The Lord will provide': often said as a shallow cliché, that simple statement contains a deep, remarkable truth. It is a truth experienced when instead of pleading lack of resources, insufficient funds or being distracted by 'fleeting and temporal things', we truly seek first the kingdom of God. We experience it when faith takes reasonable risks; when prayer seeks, speaks and listens; when God really is put first. The Lord is my shepherd. I shall not want.

Read
Psalms 23—24

Pray
Lord, lead us to still waters, lay a table before us, make cups overflow.

•••••†•••••

16 Jan, 17 May, 16 Sep

Chapter 3: Summoning the community for counsel

As often as anything important is to be done in the monastery, the prioress or abbot shall call the whole community together and explain what the business is; and after hearing the advice of the members, let them ponder it and follow what they judge the wiser course. The reason why we have said all should be called for counsel is that the Spirit often reveals what is better to the younger. The community members, for their part, are to express their opinions with all humility, and not presume to defend their own views obstinately. The decision is rather the prioress' or the abbot's to make, so that when the abbot or prioress of the community has determined what is more prudent, all must obey. Nevertheless, just as it is proper for disciples to obey their teacher, so it is becoming for the teacher to settle everything with foresight and fairness.

Reflection

Wouldn't it be wonderful if staff meetings at work were like this? Or if the church AGM changed from 'Awfully Gruesome Moanings' to being 'About God Mainly'?

Imagine if they were occasions where business was clearly explained, where opinions were voiced humbly and cooperatively and the advice of all the people was listened to – regardless of age or experience. For it is through that process and the working of the Spirit that decisions and progress are made. Simple.

Of course, the reality is very different. However, even if people do not agree with the final decision, if they feel they have had a chance to speak and have been listened to, they are more likely to go along with it.

In what ways might this approach make a difference in your church or workplace?

Read
Psalm 25

Pray
Lord Jesus, may I truly value the opinions of others even when I disagree with them.

·····✝·····

17 Jan, 18 May, 17 Sep

Chapter 3: Summoning the community for counsel

Accordingly, in every instance, all are to follow the teaching of the Rule, and no one shall rashly deviate from it. In the monastery, monastics are not to follow their own heart's desire, nor shall they presume to contend with the prioress or abbot defiantly, or outside the monastery. Should any presume to do so, let them be subjected to the discipline of the Rule. Moreover, the prioress or abbot must themselves reverence God and keep the Rule in everything they do; they can be sure beyond any doubt that they will have to give an account of all their judgments to God, the most just of judges.

If less important business of the monastery is to be transacted, the prioress and abbot shall take counsel with the elders only, as it is written: 'Do everything with counsel and you will not be sorry afterward' (Sirach 32:24).[15]

Reflection

The door bell rang. It was the water company. While the workers got on with the job they'd come to do, someone else from the water company appeared. He asked me about the service being provided and what I thought of it. We talked for a few minutes before he introduced himself as the chief executive. He was spending time with the people on the frontline, something he did one day a month, every month, spending time to find out what it's really like.

So often in businesses, organisations and churches, the leadership focus on bigger issues and leaves the 'less important business' to others. But what if, St Benedict seems to suggest, these routine issues are the real task of leaders and everything else, the really important stuff, is framed by the principle of yesterday's reading: where all are listened to, where all have a part to play? This is a community where apparent 'consultation' is not simply going through the motions to 'approve' a decision already made: a community where really listening to the people makes a real difference.

Think back to times when you have sought and received the views of others and the difference it made.

Read
Psalms 26—27

Pray
Thank you, God, for those who have helped me to listen, to learn and to understand.

18 Jan, 19 May, 18 Sep

Chapter 4: The tools for good works

First of all, 'love God with your whole heart, your whole soul and all your strength, and love your neighbour as yourself' (Matthew 22:37–39; Mark 12:30–31; Luke 10:27). Then the following: 'You are not to kill, not to commit adultery; you are not to steal nor to covet' (Romans 13:9); 'you are not to bear false witness' (Matthew 19:18; Mark 10:19; Luke 18:20). 'You must honour everyone' (1 Peter 2:17), and 'never do to another what you do not want done to yourself' (Tobit 4:15; Matthew 7:12; Luke 6:31).

'Renounce yourself in order to follow Christ' (Matthew 16:24; Luke 9:23); 'discipline your body' (1 Corinthians 9:27); do not pamper yourself, but love fasting. You must relieve the lot of the poor, 'clothe the naked, visit the sick' (Matthew 25:36), and bury the dead. Go to help the troubled and console the sorrowing.

Reflection

In this chapter, St Benedict provides some tools for the toolbox. These tools enable us to live out our faith and trust in the Lord who provides. They help us to listen, to change and to achieve stability.

The Bible is one of our tools for good works. Take just one of the above quotes from scripture and, in the silence, read it two or three times. Reflect and meditate on it for a few minutes. Mull it over, stay with it – what does it say to you?

Then respond to it – praying to God about it.

And listen for God's response.

Read
Psalms 28—29

Pray
May I always be guided by your word and your voice.

·····†·····

19 Jan, 20 May, 19 Sep

Chapter 4: The tools for good works

Your way of acting should be different from the world's way; the love of Christ must come before all else. You are not to act in anger or nurse a grudge. Rid your heart of all deceit. Never give a hollow greeting of peace or turn away when someone needs your love. Bind yourself to no oath lest it prove false, but speak the truth with heart and tongue.

'Do not repay one bad turn with another' (1 Thessalonians 5:15; 1 Peter 3:9). Do not injure anyone, but bear injuries patiently. 'Love your enemies' (Matthew 5:44; Luke 6:27). If people curse you, do not curse them back but bless them instead. 'Endure persecution for the sake of justice' (Matthew 5:10).

'You must not be proud, nor be given to wine' (Titus 1:7; 1 Timothy 3:3). Refrain from too much eating or sleeping, and 'from laziness' (Romans 12:11). Do not grumble or speak ill of others.

Reflection

'Your way of acting should be different from the world's way; the love of Christ must come before all else.'

It's easy to look upon those words from St Benedict and be daunted by such high standards; indeed, it won't be the first time that will be the case, as we take what feels like a rollercoaster ride through the *Rule* over these next few weeks.

It's natural to compare oneself with other people, to focus on our faults and to believe we can never be like that. But it is the love of Christ which is the centre of everything. Everything we do stems from that love. That love is the toolbox into which everything else sits.

Spend time thanking God for the ways in which your actions are different in a positive way.

Think about the ways in which the love of Christ comes before everything else.

Read
Psalm 30

Pray
May I always put the love of Christ before all else.

20 Jan, 21 May, 20 Sep

Chapter 4: The tools for good works

Place your hope in God alone. If you notice something good in yourself, give credit to God, not to yourself, but be certain that the evil you commit is always your own and yours to acknowledge.

Live in fear of the day of judgment and have a great horror of hell. Yearn for everlasting life with holy desire. Day by day remind yourself that you are going to die. Hour by hour keep careful watch over all you do, aware that God's gaze is upon you, wherever you may be. As soon as wrongful thoughts come into your heart, dash them against Christ and disclose them to your spiritual guide. Guard your lips from harmful or deceptive speech.

Prefer moderation in speech and speak no foolish chatter, nothing just to provoke laughter; do not love immoderate or boisterous laughter.

Reflection

We will return to the topics of talking and laughter at a later point. But for today: many people talk about 'work-life balance', but here we have the key to 'whole-life balance' – the balance between what comes from us and what comes from God.

Building on yesterday, we are allowed to feel good about ourselves. Knowing and naming those things reflects God's gaze upon us and balances out the more difficult aspects of our life and who we are. This is the balance of taking full responsibility for all we do or say which is wrong and giving God the glory for all the good within ourselves.

Read
Psalm 31

Pray
I place my hope in you alone.

21 Jan, 22 May, 21 Sep

Chapter 4: The tools for good works

Listen readily to holy reading, and devote yourself often to prayer. Every day with tears and sighs confess your past sins to God in prayer and change from these evil ways in the future.

'Do not gratify the promptings of the flesh' (Galatians 5:16); hate the urgings of self-will. Obey the orders of the prioress and abbot unreservedly, even if their own conduct – which God forbid – be at odds with what they say. Remember the teachings of the Holy One: 'Do what they say, not what they do' (Matthew 23:3).

Do not aspire to be called holy before you really are, but first be holy that you may more truly be called so. Live by God's commandments every day; treasure chastity, harbour neither hatred nor jealousy of anyone, and do nothing out of envy. Do not love quarrelling; shun arrogance. Respect the elders and love the young. Pray for your enemies out of love for Christ. If you have a dispute with someone, make peace with that person before the sun goes down.

And finally, never lose hope in God's mercy.

These, then, are the tools of the spiritual craft. When we have used them without ceasing day and night and have returned them on the day of judgment our wages will be the reward God has promised: 'What the eye has not seen nor the ear heard, God has prepared for those who love' (1 Corinthians 2:9).

The workshop where we are to toil faithfully at all these tasks is the enclosure of the monastery and stability in the community.

Reflection

As we've seen, there are many tools in St Benedict's toolbox:

- Holy reading – or *lectio divina*[16]
- Prayer
- Confession – and change from past behaviour
- Resisting the temptations of self-will
- Listening to the teachings of others
- Living in a holy way
- Fidelity in relationships
- Controlling anger
- Respecting other people
- Making peace with others
- Hope in God's mercy

When we open a toolbox, we may only pick out one tool at a time. We use it, put it back and then choose another one. We don't always know how to use a tool straight away – it can take practice. As Brother Lawrence wrote in response to a letter he had received: 'She seems to me full of good will, but she would go faster than grace. One does not become holy all at once.'[17] We can learn and practise our skills and, yes, it's okay: we won't get it right all the time.

Take one of the tools from those shown above and focus on how you might use it.

Read
Psalm 32

Pray
Help me to use the tools you have given me.

22 Jan, 23 May, 22 Sep

Chapter 5: Obedience

The first step of humility is unhesitating obedience, which comes naturally to those who cherish Christ above all. Because of the holy service they have professed, or because of dread of hell and for the glory of everlasting life, they carry out the orders of the prioress or abbot as promptly as if the command came directly from God. The Holy One says of people like this: 'No sooner did they hear than they obeyed me' (Psalm 18:44); again, God tells teachers: 'Whoever listens to you, listens to me' (Luke 10:16). Such people as these immediately put aside their own concerns, abandon their own will, and lay down whatever they have in hand, leaving it unfinished. With the ready step of obedience, they follow the voice of authority in their actions. Almost at the same moment, then, as the teacher gives the instruction the disciple quickly puts it into practice out of reverence for God; and both actions together are swiftly completed as one.

It is love that impels them to pursue everlasting life; therefore, they are eager to take the narrow road of which God says: 'Narrow is the road that leads to life' (Matthew 7:14). They no longer live by their own judgment, giving in to their whims and appetites; rather they walk according

to another's decisions and directions, choosing to live in monasteries and to have a prioress or abbot over them. Monastics of this resolve unquestionably conform to the saying of Christ: I have come not to do my own will, but the will of the One who sent me' (John 6:38).

Reflection

St Benedict considers humility in much more depth in chapter 7 of the *Rule*, but we see here a clear marker that obedience – listening to God – is of primary importance in the life of a believer. In all things we are to abandon our own will and desires and follow the words of God, which lead us to experience life in all its fullness.

When we embark on a long journey, there are certain stages which might be fairly straightforward – take the M5 to junction 30, for example. But what actually matters are the more precise and detailed instructions which enable us to reach our actual destination – then take the A road, second exit at the roundabout, left at the crossroads, up the hill and around the bend and it's the first entrance on the right. If we don't listen to the directions or think we know a better route, we may get lost.

Listening to God's loving instructions enables us not only to find but also to travel the narrow road: the road that leads to life.

Read
Psalm 33

Pray
Help me to listen to you at all times and in all places.

23 Jan, 24 May, 23 Sep

Chapter 5: Obedience

This very obedience, however, will be acceptable to God and agreeable to people only if compliance with what is commanded is not cringing or sluggish or half-hearted, but free from any grumbling or any reaction of unwillingness. For the obedience shown to an abbot or prioress is given to God, who has said: 'Whoever listens to you, listens to me' (Luke 10:16). Furthermore, the disciples' obedience must be given gladly, for 'God loves a cheerful giver' (2 Corinthians 9:7). If disciples obey grudgingly and grumble, not only aloud but also in their hearts, then, even though the order is carried out, their actions will not be accepted with favour by God, who sees that they are grumbling in their hearts. These disciples will have no reward for service of this kind; on the contrary, they will incur punishment for grumbling, unless they change for the better and make amends.

Reflection

'Some people are always grumbling because roses have thorns; I am thankful that thorns have roses.'[18] The propensity to grumble is intrinsic to the human condition. Of course, it takes far less thought and effort to complain and moan than it does to praise and encourage. Yet the conscious effort to invoke the latter set of attitudes is usually more rewarding and fulfilling for both giver and recipient.

Obedience to God – listening – often involves taking a new perspective: to be thankful for the thorns.

- Write a list of the people or things you grumble about.
- Give thanks for them and pray for and about them.
- Ask God to give you a new perspective.

Read
Psalm 34

Pray
Forgive my grumbling heart, Lord. May I see you in all things and all people.

·····†·····

24 Jan, 25 May, 24 Sep

Chapter 6: Restraint of speech

Let us follow the prophet's counsel: 'I said, I have resolved to keep watch over my ways that I may never sin with my tongue. I was silent and was humbled, and I refrained even from good words' (Psalm 39:1–2). Here the prophet indicates that there are times when good words are to be left unsaid out of esteem for silence. For all the more reason, then, should evil speech be curbed so that punishment for sin may be avoided. Indeed, so important is silence that permission to speak should seldom be granted even to mature disciples, no matter how good or holy or constructive their talk, because it is written: 'In a flood of words you will not avoid sin' (Proverbs 10:19); and elsewhere, 'The tongue holds the key to life and death' (Proverbs 18:21). Speaking and teaching are the teacher's task; the disciple is to be silent and listen.

Therefore, any requests to an abbot or prioress should be made with all humility and respectful submission. We absolutely condemn in all places any vulgarity and gossip and talk leading to laughter, and we do not permit a disciple to engage in words of that kind.

Reflection

'Silence is a cornerstone of Benedictine life and spiritual development,' writes Joan Chittister. 'The Rule does not call for absolute silence; it calls for thoughtful talk.'[19]

Many people find silence in conversation difficult. We can feel embarrassed or awkward if we can't think what to say, as if it was always necessary to fill the gap. We can tend to be thinking of what we are going to say next rather than listening to what's being said to us. And yet, allowing silence shows we are listening and have taken time to consider our response. Considered responses are often made up of fewer, more wisely chosen words.

'Listen' is an anagram of 'silent'. Listening requires silence and silence enables us to listen.

Think back over the past 24 hours: when might it have been better to have stayed silent?

Read
Psalm 35

Pray
Help me to listen more than to speak.

25 Jan, 26 May, 25 Sep

Chapter 7: Humility

Sisters and Brothers, divine scripture calls to us saying: 'Whoever exalts themselves shall be humbled, and whoever humbles themselves shall be exalted' (Luke 14:11; 18:14). In saying this, therefore, it shows us that every exaltation is a kind of pride, which the prophet indicates has been shunned, saying: 'O God, my heart is not exalted; my eyes are not lifted up and I have not walked in the ways of the great nor gone after marvels beyond me' (Psalm 131:1). And why? 'If I had not a humble spirit, but were exalted instead, then you would treat me like a weaned child on its mother's lap' (Psalm 131:2).

Accordingly, if we want to reach the highest summit of humility, if we desire to attain speedily that exaltation in heaven to which we climb by the humility of this present life, then by our ascending actions we must set up that ladder on which Jacob in a dream saw 'angels descending and ascending' (Genesis 28:12). Without doubt, this descent and ascent can signify only that we descend by exaltation and ascend by humility. Now the ladder erected is our life on earth, and if we humble our hearts God will raise it to heaven. We may call our body and soul the sides of this ladder, into which our divine vocation has fitted the various steps of humility and discipline as we ascend.

Reflection

Using the imagery of a ladder, St Benedict helps us take some steps towards the highest summit of humility. But what is humility?

In literature, we have characters such as the 'ever so 'umble' Uriah Heep in Charles Dickens' *David Copperfield*, who was hypocritically humble. We may also come across people who put on a false humility: 'Oh, I'm really no good at that at all.' This may be genuine lack of confidence, of course, but some use apparent humility to gain sympathy or as an excuse for not doing something.

Over these next two weeks, in this, the longest chapter of the *Rule*, we will explore this complex human attribute. And as one modern-day writer put it, 'Humility is an approach to life that says, "I don't have all the answers and I want your contribution." Humility is… the acceptance of individual limitations.'[20]

What do you understand by the word 'humility'?

Read
Psalm 36

Pray
Help me to learn what being humble means and teach me how to be more so.

26 Jan, 27 May, 26 Sep

Chapter 7: Humility

The first step of humility, then, is that we keep 'the reverence of God always before our eyes' (Psalm 36:1) and never forget it. We must constantly remember everything God has commanded, keeping in mind that all who despise God will burn in hell for their sins, and all who reverence God have everlasting life awaiting them. While we guard ourselves at every moment from sins and vices of thought or tongue, of hand or foot, of self-will or bodily desire, let us recall that we are always seen by God in the heavens, that our actions everywhere are in God's sight and are reported by angels at every hour.

Reflection

In chapter 5, St Benedict described the first step of humility as 'unhesitating obedience', and in the previous chapter that the love of Christ must come before everything else. Now, we go deeper: obedience and humility are not just about being willing to listen to God, accepting our own limitations, abandoning our own wills and desires and seeing things from a new perspective. We are to move beyond words. Esther de Waal writes, 'This is total attentiveness to the presence of God.'[21] Obedience and humility are about always showing reverence to God. That is the first step. That is the starting point.

Read
Psalm 37:1–22

Pray
May all I do be in reverence to you, Lord.

·····†·····

27 Jan, 28 May, 27 Sep

Chapter 7: Humility

The prophet indicates this to us, showing that our thoughts are always present to God, saying: 'God searches hearts and minds' (Psalm 7:9); and again: 'The Holy One knows our thoughts' (Psalm 94:11); likewise, 'From afar you know my thoughts' (Psalm 139:2); and, 'My thoughts shall give you praise' (Psalm 76:10). That we may take care to avoid sinful thoughts, we must always say to ourselves: 'I shall be blameless in God's sight if I guard myself from my own wickedness' (Psalm 18:23).

Reflection

It would be very easy to think of these verses from the Psalms from a negative perspective: 'God searches…', 'the Holy One knows…' as if he is some kind of Orwellian Big Brother. But they actually speak of the love and attention God pays towards us – even right down to our most intimate thoughts. This love and attention is so deep and special: God not only knows our thoughts but he cares about them. He knows we struggle with unwanted and sometimes disturbing thoughts – those things that pop into our mind or those irrational thoughts over which we obsess and which cause distress. It is what we do with those thoughts that matters, not the thoughts themselves – hence the psalmist's counsel to guard ourselves against acting upon or developing wrongful thoughts.

In return for God's love and attention for this hidden and secret side of our humanity, our thoughts are also to be the foundation of our praise for him.

Bring before God any persistent thoughts which cause you to feel uncomfortable before him.

Read
Psalm 37:23–41

Pray
May all my thoughts be reverent to you.

·····†·····

28 Jan, 29 May, 28 Sep

Chapter 7: Humility

Truly, we are forbidden to do our own will, for scripture tells us: 'Turn away from your desires' (Sirach 18:30). And in prayer too we ask that God's 'will be done' in us (Matthew 6:10). We are rightly taught not to do our own will, since we dread what scripture says: 'There are ways which some call right that in the end plunge into the depths of hell' (Proverbs 16:25). Moreover, we fear what is said of those who ignore this: 'They are corrupt and have become depraved in their desires' (Psalm 14:1).

As for the desires of the body, we must believe that God is always with us, for 'All my desires are known to you' (Psalms 38:9), as the prophet tells God. We must then be on guard against any base desire, because death is stationed near the gateway of pleasure. For this reason, Scripture warns us, 'Pursue not your lusts' (Sirach 18:30).

Reflection

After considering our actions and our thoughts, St Benedict now turns to considering how our desires can lead us astray.

Everyone experiences lustful thoughts and desires, and we will be tempted by those which are inappropriate to ourselves and to those we love. Note how the writer of Sirach[22] advocates us not to *pursue* such desires. As with our thoughts, some feelings of lust are natural and unexpected, and it's how we respond or react to them that is important. It's what we do with them that counts.

Bring before God any desires you have which make you uncomfortable.

Read
Psalm 38

Pray
May all my desires be reverent to you.

·····✝·····

29 Jan, 30 May, 29 Sep

Chapter 7: Humility

> Accordingly, if 'the eyes of God are watching the good and the wicked' (Proverbs 15:3), if at all times 'the Holy One looks down from the heavens on us to see whether we understand and seek God' (Psalm 14:2); and if every day the angels assigned to us report our deeds to God day and night, then, we must be vigilant every hour or, as the prophet says in the Psalm, God may observe us 'falling' at some time into evil and 'so made worthless' (Psalm 14:3). After sparing us for a while because God is loving and waits for us to improve, we may be told later, 'This you did, and I said nothing' (Psalm 50:21).

Reflection

This first step of humility has focused on being aware that God watches over our actions and knows our innermost thoughts and desires. We all make mistakes, and God may choose to allow us to fall in order that we may learn. Oprah Winfrey once said, 'Being human means you will make mistakes. And you will make mistakes, because failure is God's way of moving you in another direction.'[23]

Think back on just one of your mistakes – what did you learn from it?

Read
Psalm 39

Pray
May all my mistakes increase my reverence to you.

·····†·····

30 Jan, 31 May, 30 Sep

Chapter 7: Humility

> The second step of humility is that we love not our own will nor take pleasure in the satisfaction of our desires; rather we shall imitate by our actions that saying of Christ's: 'I have come not to do my own will, but the will of the One who sent me' (John 6:38). Similarly, we read, 'Consent merits punishment; constraint wins a crown.'

Reflection

The second step reiterates and reinforces the first: deepening our ambition to live a life that is committed to showing reverence, and abandoning our own will so that it is aligned with that of God's.

The last, slightly enigmatic statement, sees St Benedict quoting from the martyr Anastasia.[24] Peter Funk OSB observes: 'In this connection we see how even allowing for obedience under unjust circumstances can be more fruitful than following our own inner light, for this docility allows God to act and conforms us more closely to Christ Himself.'[25] David Foster develops this point further: 'We need to want what God wants, not what we want, or perhaps better, we need to want because God wants it, not because we want it.'[26]

Discerning any differences between God's will and our own is sometimes hard. What insights have you gained in your lifetime which have helped you determine what God wants?

Read
Psalm 40

Pray
'I delight to do your will, O my God' (Psalm 40:8).

·····†·····

31 Jan, 1 Jun, 1 Oct

Chapter 7: Humility

The third step of humility is that we submit to the prioress or abbot in all obedience for the love of God, imitating Jesus Christ of whom the apostle says: 'Christ became obedient even to death' (Philippians 2:8).

Reflection

Once again, the steps of humility reiterate and reinforce the previous ones, but this one reminds us to obey – to listen to – those who are our leaders.

'For Benedict, a superior is simply someone over us – not someone better than us, not someone who knows more than we do and for sure not necessarily anyone more holy than we,' writes Philip

Lawrence OSB.[27] And where they are leaders moulded in the way that previous chapters have guided, we ought to be able to put our trust in them not to abuse this definition of being superior.

But – and here's the rub – whether at work, church or elsewhere, those in positions of leadership will ask us to do things we are happy to do as well as things we do not want to do. How obedient are we to be then? Nothing will ever equate with Christ's obedience to death on the cross, but there will be times when we are sorely tried, when humility takes us to the edge.

Think about an occasion when you didn't want to do something you were asked to do (at work, church, in family life or elsewhere). What did it teach you about the nature of obedience?

Read
Psalm 41

Pray
Please help me when obedience to other people is hard.

1 Feb, 2 Jun, 2 Oct

Chapter 7: Humility

The fourth step of humility is that in this obedience under difficult, unfavourable, or even unjust conditions, our hearts quietly embrace suffering and endure it without weakening or seeking escape. For scripture has it: 'Anyone who perseveres to the end will be saved' (Matthew 10:22), and again, 'Be brave of heart and rely on God' (Psalm 27:14). Another passage shows how the faithful must endure everything, even contradiction, for the sake of the Holy One, saying in the person of those who suffer, 'For your sake we are put to death continually; we are regarded as sheep marked for slaughter' (Romans 8:36; Psalm 44:22). They are so confident in their expectation of reward from God that they continue joyfully and say, 'But in all this we overcome because of Christ who so greatly loved us' (Romans 8:37). Elsewhere scripture says: 'O God, you have tested us, you have tried us as silver is tried by fire; you have led us into a snare, you have placed afflictions on our backs' (Psalm 66:10–11). Then, to show that we ought to be under a prioress or an abbot, it adds: 'You have placed others over our heads' (Psalm 66:12).

In truth, those who are patient amid hardships and unjust treatment are fulfilling God's command: 'When struck on one cheek, they turn the other; when deprived of their coat, they offer their cloak also; when pressed into service for one mile, they go two' (Matthew 5:39–41). With the apostle Paul, they bear with 'false companions, endure persecution, and bless those who curse them' (2 Corinthians 11:26; 1 Corinthians 4:12).

Reflection

If we have not already got the message, St Benedict now reminds us that obedience and humility are hard. Doing what God wants us to do and listening to him with all that is going on around us are tough. This may mean, for example, not succumbing to peer pressure, or not accepting a job offer when others expect you to, because you know it's not what God is saying.

Think back to times when you have been in difficult, unfavourable or even unjust conditions. What helped you to continue listening to God in those periods?

Read
Psalms 42—43

Pray
Help me to be obedient in times of difficulty.

2 Feb, 3 Jun, 3 Oct

Chapter 7: Humility

> The fifth step of humility is that we do not conceal from the abbot or prioress any sinful thoughts entering our hearts, or any wrongs committed in secret, but rather confess them humbly. Concerning this, scripture exhorts us: 'Make known your way to the Holy One and hope in God' (Psalm 37:5). And again, 'Confess to the Holy One, for goodness and mercy endure forever' (Psalm 106:1; Psalm 118:1). So too the prophet: 'To you I have acknowledged my offence; my faults I have not concealed. I have said: Against myself I will report my faults to you, and you have forgiven the wickedness of my heart' (Psalm 32:5–6).

Reflection

In *The Picture of Dorian Gray*, Oscar Wilde writes, 'It is the confession, not the priest, that gives us absolution.'[28] He may well have been right; there is value in being able to confess what we have done wrong to another person. Indeed, the familiar old Scottish proverb, 'Open confession is good for the soul', echoes the value of talking to someone about things we have done wrong. In doing so, we humble ourselves before someone else: awkward, embarrassing, humiliating – yes. But there is also something deeply healing when we do so.

Reflect upon a time when you saw the benefits of admitting you were wrong.

Read
Psalm 44

Pray
Thank you that you understand when I make mistakes.

·····†·····

3 Feb, 4 Jun, 4 Oct

Chapter 7: Humility

The sixth step of humility is that we are content with the lowest and most menial treatment, and regard ourselves as a poor and worthless worker in whatever task we are given, saying: 'I am insignificant and ignorant, no better than a beast before you, yet I am with you always' (Psalm 73:22–23).

Reflection

Many people might align themselves with this particular part of the definition of humility. In some respects, this is probably the most comfortable step as we climb this twelve-rung ladder.

Even in those times when we feel badly treated, insignificant and no better than anyone or anything else, we are always with God. And God is always with us.

Keep silent for a while and meditate on that astonishing fact: that you are always with God and God is always with you.

Read
Psalms 45—46

Pray
Thank you, God, that you are always present.

4 Feb, 5 Jun, 5 Oct

Chapter 7: Humility

> The seventh step of humility is that we not only admit with our tongues but are also convinced in our hearts that we are inferior to all and of less value, humbling ourselves and saying with the prophet: 'I am truly a worm, not even human, scorned and despised by all' (Psalm 22:6). 'I was exalted, then I was humbled and overwhelmed with confusion' (Psalm 88:16). And again, 'It is a blessing that you have humbled me so that I can learn your commandments' (Psalm 119:71, 73).

Reflection

'Pride comes before a fall.' Whether it is our political leaders or childhood television heroes, how often have we seen the powerful brought down by events or past misdemeanours? Other times, we can be reminded of our own relative unimportance. Consider the story of an American president who, every evening, would walk out to his garden and look up at the stars in the night sky, simply to remind himself how insignificant he really was.

Humbling ourselves and being humbled by circumstances provide valuable perspectives on just how precious we are to God.

Recall a time when you were humbled by circumstances. What feelings rose up within you?

Read
Psalms 47—48

Pray
Help me, Lord, to know my place.

·····†·····

5 Feb, 6 Jun, 6 Oct

Chapter 7: Humility

The eighth step of humility is that we do only what is endorsed by the common Rule of the monastery and the example set by the prioress or abbot.

Reflection

Learning from others is an integral part of who we are as human beings. As children, we learn from parental figures and school teachers. As adults, we learn from those who train us how to do a job. Our peers and elders at all stages of life can have an influence. We may also learn from those of previous generations who committed their knowledge in writing for us to read, learn and inwardly digest. It's also the case, as someone once said, that 'the people who influenced me most are the ones who didn't try to'.

So this eighth step of humility reminds us that the words and actions of others can have an important influence on how we act and behave individually and with others. These influences are to be carried carefully and checked with those we respect and continue to learn from. Such common understanding aids purpose, respect, growth and stability.

Who are the people who have influenced you the most?

Read
Psalm 49

Pray
Thank you, Lord, for the people I have learned from.

·····†·····

6 Feb, 7 Jun, 7 Oct

Chapter 7: Humility

> The ninth step of humility is that we control our tongues and remain silent, not speaking unless asked a question, for scripture warns, 'In a flood of words you will not avoid sinning' (Proverbs 10:19), and, 'A talkative person goes about aimlessly on earth' (Psalm 140:11).

Reflection

As we explored in chapter 6 (see p. 52), many people feel uncomfortable with silence. Add to the conversational mix being interrupted, talked over or misunderstood, and we can struggle to feel we have been listened to, respected, valued and cared for.

Think about those times when you have talked to someone and they said nothing or little in response but simply listened.

Read
Psalm 50

Pray
Help me to listen to people more carefully.

·····†·····

7 Feb, 8 Jun, 8 Oct

Chapter 7: Humility

> **The tenth step of humility is that we are not given to ready laughter, for it is written: 'Only fools raise their voices in laughter' (Sirach 21:20).**

Reflection

Whether it's Laurel and Hardy or Morecambe and Wise, Victoria Wood or Michael McIntyre, having a good laugh has been shown to improve pain tolerance and decrease stress and is good for our physical and mental well-being. Nowadays, even preachers are encouraged to use some of the skills employed by stand-up comedians… Okay, so it may not always work, but humour keeps people's attention. We learn better if we engage with the message in a variety of ways.

Humour has another place in our psyche also. We may know people who crack jokes and are the life and soul of the office or the club, but it actually masks a lack of confidence about just being themselves.

Laughter is an important part of who we are and is one of God's many gifts to us. So, in what ways does humour aid our humility?

Read
Psalm 51

Pray
May my sense of humour be reverent, Lord, and honouring to others.

·····✝·····

8 Feb, 9 Jun, 9 Oct

Chapter 7: Humility

> **The eleventh step of humility is that we speak gently and without laughter, seriously and with becoming modesty, briefly and reasonably, but without raising our voices, as it is written: 'The wise are known by few words.'**

Reflection

Quoting from the first-century writings of Sextus,[29] St Benedict summarises his views on the use of speech and language which have featured a lot in this and the previous chapter. Our words reflect God's love for other people. 'Our authority to speak is rooted in our ability to remain silent,' writes Barbara Brown Taylor. 'Some of the most effective language in the world leads you up to the brink of silence and leaves you there, with the soft surf of the unsayable lapping at your feet... When we run out of words, then and perhaps only then can God be God.'[30] The way we use our words speaks not only of our humility but also of God's love.

Think back over the past 24 hours and the conversations you had or heard. Which ones were like 'a noisy gong or a clanging cymbal' and which used words demonstrating that the 'greatest is love' (1 Corinthians 13)?

Read
Psalms 52—54

Pray
May my words be ones which come from love.

·····✝·····

9 Feb, 10 Jun, 10 Oct

Chapter 7: Humility

The twelfth step of humility is that we always manifest humility in our bearing no less than in our hearts, so that it is evident at the Opus Dei, in the oratory, the monastery or the garden, on a journey or in the field, or anywhere else. Whether sitting, walking or standing, our heads must be bowed and our eyes cast down. Judging ourselves always guilty on account of our sins, we should consider that we are already at the fearful judgment, and constantly say in our hearts what the publican in the gospel said with downcast eyes: 'I am a sinner, not worthy to look up to the heavens' (Luke 18:13). And with the prophet: 'I am bowed down and humbled in every way' (Psalm 38:6–8; Psalm 119:107).

Now, therefore, after ascending all these steps of humility, we will quickly arrive at the 'perfect love' of God which 'casts out fear' (1 John 4:18). Through this love, all that we once performed with dread, we will now begin to observe without effort, as though naturally, from habit, no longer out of fear of hell, but out of love for Christ, good habit and delight in virtue. All this God will by the Holy Spirit graciously manifest in us now cleansed of vices and sins.

Reflection

Joan Chittister writes that this chapter on humility 'does not say, "Be perfect." It says, "Be honest about what you are and you will come to know God."'[31] 'It is growth into a relationship of love,' adds Esther de Waal. 'The key to my growth in humility is that humility brings me closer to God as it subjects me more and more to the pull of the gravitational force of God's love… so that love gains more and more possession of my soul.'[32]

Reflecting on these twelve steps, how has your understanding of your own humility before God and other people changed?

Read
Psalms 55—56

Pray
Lord, bring me closer and closer to your perfect love.

10 Feb, 11 Jun, 11 Oct

Chapter 8: The Divine Office at night

During the winter season, that is, from the first of November until Easter, it seems reasonable to arise at the eighth hour of the night. By sleeping until a little past the middle of the night, the community can arise with their food fully digested. In the time remaining after Vigils, those who need to learn some of the psalter or readings should study them.

Between Easter and the first of November mentioned above, the time for Vigils should be adjusted so that a very short interval after Vigils will give the members opportunity to care for nature's needs. Then, at daybreak, Lauds should follow immediately.

Reflection

Having laid the foundations, the *Rule* now takes us to the core of life with St Benedict: the Opus Dei (Work of God). These next few chapters of the *Rule* provide detailed instructions on when to pray, how to worship using hymns and psalms, and ways to learn from God through scripture and other writings.[33]

We begin our exploration of the Work of God at night. Now, unless you live in a monastic community or work a night shift, the practice of Vigils at two o'clock in the morning is unlikely to be part of your daily routine. But if you are someone who doesn't sleep well or are prone to lying awake worrying, then to have some form of prayer to hand may well be helpful. It could be just a single verse or short prayer or even a single word, such as 'Maranatha' ('Come, O Lord') to repeat to yourself, or you could sing a Taizé song, chorus or hymn inwardly and quietly.

What might your Vigils look like?

Read
Psalms 57—58

Pray
Give me your peace and presence at night, Lord.

·····✝·····

11 Feb, 12 Jun, 12 Oct

Chapter 9: The number of psalms at the Night Office

During the winter season, Vigils begin with the verse: 'O God, open my lips and my mouth shall proclaim your praise' (Psalm 51:16). After this has been said three times, the following order is observed: Psalm 3 with Doxology; Psalm 9 with a refrain, or at least chanted; an Ambrosian hymn; then six Psalms with refrain.

After the Psalmody, a versicle is said and the prioress or abbot gives a blessing. When all are seated on the benches, the members in turn read three selections from the book on the lectern. After each reading a responsory is sung. The Doxology is not sung after the first two responsories, but only after the third reading. As soon as the cantor begins to sing the Doxology, let all rise from their seats in honour and reverence for the Holy Trinity. Besides the inspired books of the Old and New Testaments, the works read at Vigils should include explanations of scripture by reputable and orthodox writers.

When these three readings and their responsories have been finished, the remaining six Psalms are sung with the 'alleluia' refrain. This ended, there follow a reading from the apostle recited by heart, a versicle and the litany, that is, 'Christ, have mercy'. And so Vigils are concluded.

Reflection

What a wonderful way to begin the day: to get up, sit on the edge of the bed and say: 'O God, open my lips and my mouth shall proclaim your praise' – not once, but three times. This is an exercise in setting the day before the Lord: a day to sing his praise – no matter what those hours may bring. As Bishop Michael Perham once said, 'There is, in a sense, nothing in it for me. It is all for Him, the Father who opens our lips that our mouths may proclaim His praise.'[34]

We will return to the centrality of the Psalms in due course but also crucial to the Work of God in our lives each day is time to read the Bible and the writings of the early church teachers.[35] We have much to learn from the people who were living at a time which was closer to the founding of the Christian church and who were at the forefront of understanding, exploring and developing the faith.

So, here are two practical ways to enhance our own spiritual way of living: beginning the day with a word from God and learning from the words of others.

From now on, how about starting each day by saying those words from Psalm 51?

Read
Psalms 59—60

Pray
O God, open my lips and my mouth shall proclaim your praise.

12 Feb, 13 Jun, 13 Oct

Chapter 10: The arrangement of the Night Office in summer

From Easter until the first of November, the winter arrangement for the number of Psalms is followed. But because summer nights are shorter, the readings from the book are omitted. In place of the three readings, one from the Old Testament is substituted. This is to be recited by heart, followed by a short responsory. In everything else, the winter arrangement for Vigils is kept. Thus, winter and summer, there are never fewer than twelve Psalms at Vigils, not counting Psalms 3 and 94.

Reflection

Not to be confused with Night Prayer (or Compline), to which we will return later, the Night Office of Vigils acknowledges the changes in the seasons and times of year in a very practical way. A shorter night means a shorter office. This is a recognition that even the most devoted need sleep to ensure both the work and prayer of God is carried out.

You may like to revisit the entries for the past two days and reflect on how your thoughts have begun to develop.

Read
Psalms 61—62

Pray
Lord, teach me to pray.

·····†·····

13 Feb, 14 Jun, 14 Oct

Chapter 11: The celebration of Vigils on Sunday

On Sunday the community should arise earlier for Vigils. In these Vigils, too, there must be moderation in quantity: first, as we have already indicated, six Psalms are said, followed by a versicle. Then the members, seated on the benches and arranged in their proper order, listen to four readings from the book. After each reading a responsory is sung, but the Doxology is added only to the fourth. When the cantor begins it, all immediately rise in reverence.

After these readings the same order is repeated: six more Psalms with refrain as before, a versicle, then four more readings and their responsories, as above. Next, three canticles from the prophets, chosen by the prioress or abbot, are said with an 'alleluia' refrain. After a versicle and the blessing of the abbot or prioress, four New Testament readings follow with their responsories, as above. After the fourth responsory, the prioress or abbot begins the hymn 'We praise you, God'. When that is finished, they read from the gospels while all stand with respect and awe. At the conclusion of the gospel reading, all reply 'Amen', and immediately the prioress or abbot intones the hymn 'To you be praise'. After a final blessing, Lauds begin.

This arrangement for Sunday Vigils should be followed at all times, summer and winter, unless – God forbid – the members happen to arise too late. In that case, the readings or responsories will have to be shortened. Let special care be taken that this not happen, but if it does, the one at fault is to make due satisfaction to God in the oratory.

Reflection

Let's be honest, most of us would probably not choose to get up in the night for 13 readings and 15 psalms and canticles! But one point to consider in today's reading from the *Rule* is that Sundays were made to be different, to be a day dedicated to God. We need our sabbath moments.

Over the past 30 years, in the UK at least, there has been a significant increase in the number of people who work on Sunday – and a lot of them don't have a choice about that. In that same period, the number of people attending church has dropped as other activities and lifestyle changes attract attention, time and personal preference. For many people, Sundays have become like any other day in the week.

The practicalities of work and family life may also mean that the sabbath isn't necessarily on a Sunday. The important thing remains, though: to have a day of rest, a day that is different.

Do you have a day that is different? What makes it so?

Read
Psalms 63—64

Pray
May I make time to keep one day a week special.

14 Feb, 15 Jun, 15 Oct

Chapter 12: The celebration of the solemnity of Lauds

Sunday Lauds begin with Psalm 67, said straight through without a refrain. Then Psalm 51 follows with an 'alleluia' refrain. Lauds continue with Psalms 118 and 63, the Canticle of the Three Young Men, Psalms 148 through 150, a reading from the Apocalypse[36] recited by heart and followed by a responsory, an Ambrosian hymn, a versicle, the gospel canticle, the litany and the conclusion.

Reflection

Following straight on from Vigils on a Sunday, Lauds (or Morning Prayer) continue the focus on dedicating the day to God with psalms praising his name and speaking of his strength and power. These are reminders that no matter what happens, God is there and his name can be praised.

This central truth is dramatically illustrated by the Canticle of the Three Young Men.[37] Located in the events which come between Daniel 3:23 and 24, this is a song of worship to God sung in the most desperate of circumstances, for the three young men are Shadrach, Meshach and Abednego.

Standing at the beginning of a new day, or a new week, whatever 'fiery furnace' surrounds us we can praise God. The 'furnace' won't necessarily stop 'burning' or hurting us, but praising God in the midst of it can help us in our attempts to survive it. Difficult things happen. As Nadia Bolz-Weber puts it, 'The mother hen of God doesn't keep us from the danger of the fox. The mother hen offers us a place of shelter and love so we know where we belong. The fox still exists. The danger is not optional. Fear is. Under the protective wings we are loved.'[38]

Recall a time when you were able to praise God in a time of difficulty.

Read
Psalms 65—66

Pray
When things are difficult, thank you, God, that you are with me.

·····†·····

15 Feb, 16 Jun, 16 Oct

Chapter 13: The celebration of Lauds on ordinary days

On ordinary weekdays, Lauds are celebrated as follows. First, Psalm 67 is said without a refrain and slightly protracted as on Sunday so that everyone can be present for Psalm 51, which has a refrain. Next, according to custom, two more Psalms are said in the following order: on Monday, Psalms 6 and 36; on Tuesday, Psalms 43 and 57; on Wednesday, Psalms 64 and 65; on Thursday, Psalms 88 and 90; on Friday, Psalms 76 and 92; on Saturday, Psalm 143 and the Canticle from Deuteronomy,[39] divided into two sections, with the Doxology after each section. On other days, however, a Canticle from the prophets is said, according to the practice of the Roman Church. Next follow Psalms 148 through 150, a reading from the apostle recited by heart, a responsory, an Ambrosian hymn, a versicle, the Gospel canticle, the litany and conclusion.

Reflection

As we have already observed, the psalms are central to Benedictine spirituality. Ambrose Tinsley OSB writes, 'One should read each line [of a psalm] as if it were an item on a menu. Each in fact has been prepared with care, and down the ages, tried and polished and, moreover, has been found by many people to contain a flavour of its own. But then when we have spent some time with each suggestion on the menu, we may find that our own eyes are constantly returning to the one which has attracted us most. That is the one to choose and then to sit with and enjoy. We can digest it slowly and indeed, not only there and then, but also in a quiet way throughout the hours which are to come.'[40]

Take the time to read Psalm 67: the one with which Lauds always start.

Which verse or word whets your appetite? Sit with it. Digest it. Live from it.

Read
Psalm 67

Pray
Make your face to shine upon me, O Lord.

16 Feb, 17 Jun, 17 Oct

Chapter 13: The celebration of Lauds on ordinary days

Assuredly, the celebration of Lauds and Vespers must never pass by without the prioress or abbot reciting the entire Prayer of Jesus at the end for all to hear, because thorns of contention are likely to spring up. Thus warned by the pledge they make to one another in the very words of this prayer: 'Forgive us as we forgive' (Matthew 6:12), they may cleanse themselves of this kind of vice. At other celebrations, only the final part of this prayer is said aloud, that all may reply: 'But deliver us from evil' (Matthew 6:13).

Reflection

Central to any period of prayer is the one which Jesus taught his disciples and which contains some of the most well-known words in the Christian faith. Whichever version you prefer, say the Lord's Prayer slowly, phrase by phrase. Use each line as a way in to further prayer.

Go for a walk and say the Lord's Prayer as you do so. Or go to your church or workplace and walk around that place saying the Lord's Prayer for all those who also belong there.

Read
Psalm 68:1–17

Pray
Our Father...

·····†·····

17 Feb, 18 Jun, 18 Oct

Chapter 14: The celebration of Vigils on the anniversaries of saints

On the feasts of saints, and indeed on all solemn festivals, the Sunday order of celebrations is followed, although the Psalms, refrains and readings proper to the day itself are said. The procedure, however, remains the same as indicated above.

Reflection

People vary in their views about saints. Some pray to saints; others ask saints to pray for them. Many churches and countries, peoples and professions have a patron saint. All those given the title 'saint' have in some way or other been shown to have lived a godly life, often one which has been benevolent to others and linked to significant change or miracles. Many saints have remarkable stories told about them – and while some accounts are hard for our 21st-century intellects to believe, there is often much to learn from the lives of those we call saints.

Take time to read about the patron saint of your church or country – or one of the more recent ones like St Maximilian Kolbe. What is it about their faithfulness and obedience to God that inspires or challenges you?

Read
Psalm 68:18–35

Pray

I give you thanks, Lord, for the lives of all saints and believers.

18 Feb, 19 Jun, 19 Oct

Chapter 15: The times for saying alleluia

From the holy feast of Easter until Pentecost, 'Alleluia' is always said with both the Psalms and the responsories. Every night from Pentecost until the beginning of Lent, it is said only with the last six Psalms of Vigils. Vigils, Lauds, Prime, Terce, Sext and None are said with 'Alleluia' every Sunday except in Lent; at Vespers, however, a refrain is used. 'Alleluia' is never said with responsories except from Easter to Pentecost.

Reflection

Alleluia! A transliteration of the Hebrew word *hallelujah*, meaning 'Praise the Lord', 'alleluia' came into use in the ancient *Liturgy of St James*, commonly attributed to James, the son of Mary and Joseph, and recognised by many as the author of the eponymous New Testament letter.

Alleluia! – described by the early Christians as 'a superlative expression of thanksgiving, joy and triumph'.

Alleluia! – a wonderful attempt to put into words that which words cannot express.

Sing or listen to a hymn or song which begins with 'Alleluia'.

Read
Psalm 69:1–23

Pray
Use the song or hymn you have chosen to sing praise to God.

19 Feb, 20 Jun, 20 Oct

Chapter 16: The celebration of the Divine Office during the day

The prophet says: 'Seven times a day have I praised you' (Psalm 119:164). We will fulfil this sacred number of seven if we satisfy our obligations of service at Lauds, Prime, Terce, Sext, None, Vespers and Compline, for it was of these hours during the day that it was said: 'Seven times a day have I praised you' (Psalm 119:164). Concerning Vigils, the same prophet says: 'At midnight I arose to give you praise' (Psalm 119:62). Therefore, we should 'praise our Creator for just judgments' at these times: Lauds, Prime, Terce, Sext, None, Vespers and Compline; and 'Let us arise at night to give praise' (Psalm 119:62, 164).

Reflection

'We have to acknowledge that there is no set number of Psalms or prayer times that is automatically pleasing to God. What is essential, though, is that the Office be carried out reverently and regularly. Heartfelt prayer is the goal, so that God may be worshipped and the participants be led to the Maker of all.'[41]

For praise to become part of our rhythm of life, it needs to become as natural as, for example, the time we sit down for a meal. We can praise God at any time of the day and the duration will follow. Firstly, it's about getting into a routine, a pattern, a rhythm of setting aside the time for giving intentional attention to God.

'Worship is a two-way traffic,' says Michael Perham. 'The giving of praise and the receiving of grace. We offer the one. God offers the other. Worship is for the creator, yet it feeds not him, but us.'[42]

What is a good time of day for you? When are you most alert or less tired? How does it fit with the rest of your daily routine?

Read
Psalm 69:24–38

Pray
May my words be ones of constant praise.

······†······

20 Feb, 21 Jun, 21 Oct

Chapter 17: The number of psalms to be sung at these hours

We have already established the order for Psalmody at Vigils and Lauds. Now let us arrange the remaining hours.

Three Psalms are to be said at Prime, each followed by 'Glory be.' The hymn for this hour is sung after the opening versicle, 'God, come to my assistance' (Psalm 70:1), before the Psalmody begins. One reading follows the three Psalms, and the hour is concluded with a versicle, 'Lord, have mercy' and the dismissal.

Prayer is celebrated in the same way at Terce, Sext and None: that is, the opening verse, the hymn appropriate to each hour, three Psalms, a reading with a versicle, 'Lord, have mercy' and the dismissal. If the community is rather large, refrains are used with the Psalms; if it is smaller, the Psalms are said without refrain.

At Vespers the number of Psalms should be limited to four, with refrain. After these Psalms there follow: a reading and responsory, an Ambrosian hymn, a versicle, the Gospel Canticle, the litany, and, immediately before the dismissal, the Lord's Prayer.

Compline is limited to three Psalms without refrain. After the Psalmody comes the hymn for this hour, followed by a reading a versicle, 'Lord, have mercy,' a blessing and the dismissal.

Reflection

A common way of ending a psalm is to say or sing a doxology such as:

Glory be to the Father and to the Son and to the Holy Spirit;
as it was in the beginning, is now and shall be forever. Amen.

This is a seemingly simple set of words, but they are ones which encompass the whole Trinitarian nature of God across the whole span of time that ever was and ever will be. They are words to say when our own words fall short of fully expressing our thoughts on God's glory.

This book provides a reading from the Psalms for you to read every day. Why not say the one for today out loud and end it by saying the words of this glory-giving doxology?

Read
Psalm 70

Pray
Whatever I do, Lord, where possible, may it be to your glory.

·····✝·····

21 Feb, 22 Jun, 22 Oct

Chapter 18: The order of the psalmody

> Each of the day hours begins with the verse, 'O God, come to my assistance; O God, make haste to help me' (Psalm 70:1), followed by the Doxology and the appropriate hymn.
>
> Then, on Sunday at Prime, four sections of Psalm 119 are said. At the other hours, that is, at Terce, Sext and None, three sections of this Psalm are said. On Monday three Psalms are said at Prime: Psalms 1, 2 and 6. At Prime each day thereafter until Sunday, three Psalms are said in consecutive order as far as Psalm 20. Psalms 9 and 18 are each divided into two sections. In this way, Sunday Vigils can always begin with Psalm 21.

Reflection

Once again, we see the importance of saying psalms each day. Psalms are to become embedded into our very soul and being.

Saying them is to be as natural as having a drink or a meal. They can be punctuation marks in the sentences of our lives.

> Sing psalms and hymns and spiritual songs among yourselves,
> singing and making melody to the Lord in your hearts, giving
> thanks to God the Father at all times.
> EPHESIANS 5:19–20

If you were to choose a psalm or verses from a psalm which are particularly special to you, which would it be? Why is it special?

Read
Psalm 71

Pray
Take words from your chosen psalm and make it your prayer.

·····✝·····

22 Feb, 23 Jun, 23 Oct

Chapter 18: The order of the psalmody

On Monday at Terce, Sext and None, the remaining nine sections of Psalm 119 are said, three sections at each hour. Psalm 119 is thus completed in two days, Sunday and Monday. On Tuesday, three Psalms are said at each of the hours of Terce, Sext and None. These are the nine Psalms, 120—128. The same Psalms are repeated at these hours daily up to Sunday. Likewise, the arrangement of hymns, readings and versicles for these days remains the same. In this way, Psalm 119 will always begin on Sunday.

Reflection

'The Psalms express the reality of my longing for God and my joy and suffering in the vicissitudes of my search for him,' writes Esther de Waal. 'Sometimes God is close, sometimes distant. I seek him in the desert and on the mountain, in poverty and in emptiness and in waiting.'[43]

The emotional fluctuations we find in the psalms reflect the ups and downs of our own moods. There are times of sadness and times of happiness; periods when we feel exhausted and periods when we feel energised; stages when life feels good and stages in which the cracks began to show.

Choose a psalm or verses from a psalm which speak of or to your emotions. What is it that resonates so clearly?

Read
Psalm 72

Pray
Thank you, Lord, for your understanding in times of difficulty.

·····†·····

23 Feb (use page 92 in a leap year), 24 Jun, 24 Oct

Chapter 18: The order of the psalmody

Four Psalms are sung each day at Vespers, starting with Psalm 110 and ending with Psalm 147, omitting the Psalms in this series already assigned to other hours, namely, Psalms

118 through 128, Psalm 134 and Psalm 143. All the remaining Psalms are said at Vespers. Since this leaves three Psalms too few, the longer ones in the series should be divided: that is Psalms 139, 144 and 145. And because Psalm 117 is short, it can be joined to Psalm 116. This is the order of Psalms for Vespers; the rest is as arranged above: the reading, responsory, hymn, versicle and canticle. The same Psalms – 4, 91 and 134 – are said each day at Compline.

The remaining Psalms not accounted for in this arrangement for the day hours are distributed evenly at Vigils over the seven nights of the week. Longer Psalms are to be divided so that twelve Psalms are said each night.

Above all else we urge that if people find this distribution of the Psalms unsatisfactory, they should arrange whatever they judge better, provided that the full complement of one hundred and fifty Psalms is by all means carefully maintained every week, and that the series begins anew each Sunday at Vigils. For members who in a week's time say less than the full psalter with the customary canticles betray extreme indolence and lack of devotion in their service. We read, after all, that our holy ancestors, energetic as they were, did all this in a single day. Let us hope that we, lukewarm as we are, can achieve it in a whole week.

Reflection

The rhythm of the day is marked not just by the hours that punctuate its passing but in the way the day then gradually comes full circle and the night begins once again. 'Seven times will I praise you' (Psalm 119:164).

The main point of this whole chapter (and indeed the preceding ten) has been that the Psalms are integral to our prayer and worship. The

Psalms reflect the complete spectrum of the human condition and experience. They express anger, despair and fear; love, adoration and worship; questioning, doubt and trust. Psalms can take up a very special place in times of illness and difficulty, align themselves with our need for encouragement and affirmation, and provide a voice for our thanksgiving and praise.

It is no wonder that St Benedict placed them at the very centre of monastic life and that this centrality to our faith continues to this day.

Read
Psalms 73—74

Pray
Thank you, Lord, for the gift of the Psalms.

·····†·····

23 Feb (leap year)

Chapter 18: The order of the psalmody

Four Psalms are sung each day at Vespers, starting with Psalm 110 and ending with Psalm 147, omitting the Psalms in this series already assigned to other hours, namely, Psalms 118 through 128, Psalm 134 and Psalm 143. All the remaining Psalms are said at Vespers. Since this leaves three Psalms too few, the longer ones in the series should be divided: that is Psalms 139, 144 and 145. And because Psalm 117 is short, it can be joined to Psalm 116. This is the order of Psalms for Vespers; the rest is as arranged above: the reading, responsory, hymn, versicle and canticle. The same Psalms – 4, 91 and 134 – are said each day at Compline.

Reflection

The rhythm of the day is marked not just by the hours that punctuate its passing but in the way the day gradually turns full circle and the night begins once again.

Read
Psalm 73

Pray
'Seven times will I praise you.'

·····✝·····

24 Feb (leap year), 25 Jun, 25 Oct

Chapter 18: The order of the psalmody

The remaining Psalms not accounted for in this arrangement for the day hours are distributed evenly at Vigils over the seven nights of the week. Longer Psalms are to be divided so that twelve Psalms are said each night.

Above all else we urge that if people find this distribution of the Psalms unsatisfactory, they should arrange whatever they judge better, provided that the full complement of one hundred and fifty Psalms is by all means carefully maintained every week, and that the series begins anew each Sunday at Vigils. For members who in a week's time say less than the full psalter with the customary canticles betray extreme indolence and lack of devotion in their service. We read, after all, that our holy ancestors, energetic as they were, did all this in a single day. Let us hope that we, lukewarm as we are, can achieve it in a whole week.

Reflection

The main point of this whole chapter (and indeed the preceding ten) has been that the Psalms are integral to our prayer and worship. The Psalms reflect the complete spectrum of the human condition and experience. They express anger, despair and fear; love, adoration and worship; questioning, doubt and trust. Psalms can take up a very special place in times of illness and difficulty, align themselves with our need for encouragement and affirmation, and provide a voice for our thanksgiving and praise.

It is no wonder that St Benedict placed them at the very centre of monastic life and that this centrality to our faith continues to this day.

Read
Psalm 74

Pray
Thank you, Lord, for the gift of the Psalms.

·····†·····

24 Feb (ordinary year) 25 Feb (leap year), 26 Jun, 26 Oct

Chapter 19: The discipline of the psalmody

We believe that the divine presence is everywhere and 'that in every place the eyes of God are watching the good and the wicked' (Proverbs 15:3). But beyond the least doubt we should believe this to be especially true when we celebrate the divine office.

We must always remember, therefore, what the prophet says: 'Serve the Holy One with reverence' (Psalm 2:11), and again, 'Sing praise wisely' (Psalm 47:7); and, 'in the presence of the angels I will sing to you' (Psalm 138:1). Let us consider, then, how we ought to sing the Psalms in such a way that our minds are in harmony with our voices.

Reflection

The psalms were the hymns and choruses of St Benedict's day. In the modern church, we have a wealth of music that can stir our heart in worship and adoration of God. So whether your preference is for hymns ancient or modern, choruses or chants, we have many words to sing wisely before our Lord, words to sing in ways that ensure our minds are in harmony with our voices, as St Benedict puts it. We should sing psalms, hymns and songs as if we were in the very presence of God: stood face-to-face singing just for him – not for the person next to us or for the choir to which we belong, but just for God.

In what ways do you worship God?

Read
Psalms 75—76

Pray
May I worship you in ways that proclaim your worth.

25 Feb (ordinary year) 26 Feb (leap year), 27 Jun, 27 Oct

Chapter 20: Reverence in prayer

> Whenever we want to ask a favour of someone powerful, we do it humbly and respectfully, for fear of presumption. How much more important, then, to lay our petitions before the God of all with the utmost humility and sincere devotion. We must know that God regards our purity of heart and tears of compunction, not our many words. Prayer should therefore be short and pure, unless perhaps it is prolonged under the inspiration of divine grace. In community, however, prayer should always be brief; and when the prioress or abbot gives the signal, all should rise together.

Reflection

Our prayer is embedded in that which pricks our conscience. Ambrose Tinsley describes these as 'compunction moments' – times when we have 'behaved in ways which were not good and so regrettable'. He continues to describe how in our relationship with God we learn that 'to cope with our deflating moments will involve accepting and admitting our own weaknesses but that itself can often introduce a touch of healthy realism… We will not be able to receive from God all that he wants to give when there is some pretence in our relationship with him.'[44]

This combination of compunction with humility and reverence increasingly leads to a purity of heart, which is the very essence of all that becomes our prayer. 'Prayer is a gift rather than something we do,' writes David Foster. 'Prayer is… the "inside" of our faith, its heartbeat and lungs, the gift of the Spirit that God breathes into the core of our being.'[45]

Think about your compunction moments and the phrase 'purity of heart'. How do they come together with prayer?

Read
Psalm 77

Pray
Lord, teach me to pray that I may become one with you.

·····✝·····

26 Feb (ordinary year) 27 Feb (leap year), 28 Jun, 28 Oct

Chapter 21: The deans of the monastery

If the community is rather large, some chosen for their good repute and holy life should be made deans. They will take care of their groups of ten, managing all affairs according to the commandments of God and the orders of their prioress or abbot. Anyone selected as a dean should be the kind of person with whom the prioress or abbot can confidently share the burdens of office. They are to be chosen for virtuous living and wise teaching, not for their rank.

If perhaps one of these deans is found to be puffed up with any pride, and so deserving of censure, they are to be reproved once, twice and even a third time. Should they refuse to amend, they must be removed from office and replaced by another who is worthy. We prescribe the same course of action in regard to the subprioress or prior.

Reflection

The *Rule* returns briefly to the topic of leadership. In a monastic community, deans were viewed in the way that 'middle management' might be seen today. Responding to both the requirements of those whom they oversee and the demands of those who oversee them, they have a degree of power and in any situation the responsibility to use it well. Everyone assumes that managers will know what to do, and they are the first to get the blame if things go wrong. Modern-day workplaces are full of overstretched line-managers, often in post because of 'rank' or technical skill rather than innate managerial ability and often unable openly to acknowledge difficulty in their work.

Think back to chapter 2: how has your attitude towards those in leadership positions changed?

Read
Psalm 78:1–39

Pray
Help me to continue to be mindful of the demands and responsibilities carried by those in leadership.

27 Feb (ordinary year) 28 Feb (leap year), 29 Jun, 29 Oct

Chapter 22: The sleeping arrangements of monastics

Members are to sleep in separate beds. They receive bedding as provided by the prioress or abbot, suitable to monastic life.

If possible, all are to sleep in one place, but should the size of the community preclude this, they will sleep in groups of ten or twenty under the watchful care of elders. A lamp must be kept burning in the room until morning.

They sleep clothed, and girded with belts or cords; but they should remove their knives, lest they accidentally cut themselves in their sleep. Thus the members will always be ready to arise without delay when the signal is given; each will hasten to arrive at the Opus Dei before the others, yet with all dignity and decorum. The younger members should not have their beds next to each other, but interspersed among those of the elders. On arising for the Opus Dei, they will quietly encourage each other, for the sleepy like to make excuses.

Reflection

St Benedict's concern for the basic practicalities of life crops up throughout the *Rule*. Whether caused by waking babies, bad dreams, worry or noisy neighbours, a bad night's sleep affects our ability to function well the next day – especially if it becomes a long-term problem. It's quite alright to feel tired (although as St Benedict observes, it can sometimes be used as an excuse!) and resolving sleep difficulties is easier said than done at times. But paying attention to the apparently mundane aspects of how and where we sleep helps maximise our ability to live a life which is obedient, open to change and stable.

In what ways does your sleep pattern affect you?

Read
Psalm 78:40–72

Pray
In peace, I will lie down and sleep, for you alone, O Lord, make me dwell in safety (from Psalm 4:8).

·····†·····

28 Feb (ordinary year) 29 Feb (leap year), 30 Jun, 30 Oct

Chapter 23: Excommunication for faults

If monastics are found to be stubborn or disobedient or proud, if they grumble or in any way despise the holy Rule and defy the orders of the elders, they should be warned twice privately by them in accord with Christ's injunction (Matthew 18:15–16). If they do not amend, they must be rebuked publicly in the presence of everyone. But if even then they do not reform, let them be excommunicated,[46] provided that they understand the nature of this punishment. If however they lack understanding, let them undergo corporal punishment.

Reflection

Picking up a theme from chapter 2, the next eight chapters of the *Rule* focus on faults and misbehaviour and are sometimes referred to as the 'penal code of St Benedict'. He lived in times when punishment was somewhat harsher than the generally accepted norms of the 21st century – although, historically speaking, his approach was a light touch compared to some of his contemporaries and predecessors! Nevertheless, what he talks about may feel uncomfortable and unacceptable – but do stick with it: there are helpful lessons to be learnt.

The term 'three strikes and you're out' is not confined to the baseball field. Aspects of the modern-day legal system are still based upon Jesus' teaching cited here (see Matthew 18:15–20 for the full version). For example, workplace disciplinary policies often take an approach along the lines of 'verbal warning, first written warning and final written warning'. Churches are encouraged to deal with disputes alone, then to call witnesses, and then to come before the whole church in order to try to reach a solution before asking someone to leave.

But there always remains the saving grace: Jesus is a friend of the Gentiles and the tax collectors. So no matter what led the 'offender' to be challenged firstly by one person, then by two or three and then by a larger group, no matter what led them to be sent away, there is still the opportunity for them to listen, to seek forgiveness and to receive once again the love of God.

Do you need to be reconciled with someone else? What do you need to do to achieve this?

Read
Psalm 79

Pray
Lord Jesus, may I both seek and accept reconciliation with other people.

1 Mar, 1 Jul, 31 Oct

Chapter 24: Degrees of excommunication

There ought to be due proportion between the seriousness of a fault and the measure of excommunication or discipline. The prioress or abbot determines the gravity of faults.

If monastics are found guilty of less serious faults, they will not be allowed to share the common table. Members excluded from the common table will conduct themselves as follows: in the oratory they will not lead a Psalm or a refrain nor will they recite a reading until they have made satisfaction, and they will take meals alone, after the others have eaten. For instance, if the community eats at noon, they will eat in mid-afternoon; if the community' eats in mid-afternoon, they will eat in the evening, until by proper satisfaction pardon is gained.

Reflection

As also mentioned in chapter 2, St Benedict's approach is to try to ensure the punishment fits the crime. But with many misdemeanours, there is collateral damage – people not directly affected by the fault that has been committed find themselves hurt or upset by what has taken place. There is an effect on the wider community – be that church, workplace, family or social group.

While we can tell children to sit on the naughty step or that they can't watch a TV programme, such temporary punishments are less easy to implement in a group of adults. Footballers who get sent off may miss the next game or so. But what about in church, when someone does something that offends another or makes a significant mistake that affects other people? Do we take punitive action until 'by proper satisfaction pardon is gained' or adopt the teaching of Jesus we considered yesterday? And where does forgiveness sit among all that?

It may be that this reading from the *Rule* has prompted you to reflect on those with whom you need to be at one with: those you need to forgive and those whose forgiveness you need.

Read
Psalm 80

Pray
Help me to love those who have hurt me.

·····†·····

2 Mar, 2 Jul, 1 Nov

Chapter 25: Serious faults

Those guilty of a serious fault are to be excluded from both the table and the oratory. No one in the community should associate or converse with them at all. They will work alone at the tasks assigned to them, living continually in sorrow and penance, pondering that fearful judgment of the apostle: 'Such a person is handed over for the destruction of the flesh that the spirit may be saved on the day of Jesus Christ' (1 Corinthians 5:5). Let them take their food alone

in an amount and at a time the prioress or abbot considers appropriate. They should not be blessed by anyone passing by, nor should the food that is given them be blessed.

Reflection

Some of the deepest experiences in our faith come from when we have been stuck in the very depths that life encounters and then find, albeit sometimes after a long time, that God brings us to a better place. We go through (or get ourselves into) very difficult times: times without friends or support or times when, as Paul puts it, a 'destruction of the flesh' (and perhaps the mind and spirit) has taken place. It is by living in one of those 'rock bottom' places that we can be led to a realisation that the only way through is to come to God – so 'that the spirit may be saved'.

But it's not that simple, is it? It could be – but it isn't. Wherever there are people there are problems, and sometimes those problems are very significant and long-lasting. As we have considered in chapter 12, difficult things happen but ultimately it is our response that matters. As Psalm 23 says, 'we go through the valley' – but we don't have to stay in it. It can be a choice.

Consider life's difficulties as they may be for you at the moment – what choices could you make?

Read
Psalms 81—82

Pray
'I hear a voice I had not known: "I relieved your shoulder of the burden; your hands were freed from the basket. In distress you called, and I rescued you"' (Psalm 81:5–7).

·····✝·····

3 Mar, 3 Jul, 2 Nov

Chapter 26: Unauthorised association with the excommunicated

If anyone, acting without an order from the prioress or abbot, presumes to associate in any way with an excommunicated member, to converse with them or to send them a message, they should receive a like punishment of excommunication.

Reflection

You may think this chapter sounds totally inappropriate to 21st century life. Well, in some respects, it's not that far-fetched. For example, people who are suspended from their workplace because of an investigation into an accusation of misconduct are sometimes told not to have any contact with their colleagues or to visit the workplace – and vice versa. Or maybe you can think of a church situation where someone is being ostracised because of something they have done or are alleged to have done. But such isolation only serves to reinforce the pain of such accusations, particularly if false or subsequently not proven.

Perhaps you know of a situation which relates to the theme of today. How would it feel to be prohibited from having contact with anyone else?

Read
Psalm 83

Pray
I pray for those who find themselves isolated or ostracised.

·····✝·····

4 Mar, 4 Jul, 3 Nov

Chapter 27: The concern of the abbot and prioress for the excommunicated

The abbot and prioress must exercise the utmost care and concern for the wayward because 'it is not the healthy who need a physician, but the sick' (Matthew 9:12). Therefore, they ought to use every skill of a wise physician and send in senpectae, that is, mature and wise members who, under the cloak of secrecy, may support the wavering sister or brother, urge them to be humble as a way of making satisfaction, and 'console them lest they be overwhelmed by excessive sorrow' (2 Corinthians 2:7). Rather, as the apostle also says: 'let love be reaffirmed' (2 Corinthians 2:8), and let all pray for the one who is excommunicated.

It is the responsibility of the abbot or prioress to have great concern and to act with all speed, discernment and diligence in order not to lose any of the sheep entrusted to them. They should realize that they have undertaken care of the sick, not tyranny over the healthy. Let them also fear the threat of the prophet in which God says: 'What you saw to be fat you claimed for yourselves, and what was weak you cast aside' (Ezekiel 34:3–4). They are to imitate the loving example of Christ, the Good Shepherd, who left the ninety-nine sheep in the mountains and went in search of the one sheep that had strayed. So great was Christ's compassion for its weakness that 'he mercifully placed it on his sacred shoulders' and so carried it back to the flock (Luke 15:5).

Reflection

Isn't it great when people reach out to help us in difficult times, when we've lost our way and need someone to bring us back to whatever constitutes our personal sheepfold? Those modern-day senpectae – wise and mature people who reach out to support, comfort and encourage us – show us the love of Christ, and their compassion helps soothe the difficulties of weakness and troubled times.

It's often the 'little things' that mean so much in those times – a card, a phone call, the gift of a meal – but it is also the people who will simply listen or say something that is helpful and reassuring. In those times, when we are lost or in difficulty, it's often hard to pray. In such periods, that's what the church is for – when other people will do our praying for us.

Think back over your life. Who have been your senpectae? What was it that they said or did that made them such?

Read
Psalms 84—85

Pray
Thank you, Lord, for all those who have been like a shepherd to me when I was lost.

5 Mar, 5 Jul, 4 Nov

Chapter 28: Those who refuse to amend after frequent reproofs

If anyone has been reproved frequently for any fault, or even been excommunicated, yet does not amend, let that member receive a sharper punishment: that is, let that monastic feel the strokes of the rod. But if even then they do not reform, or perhaps become proud and would actually defend their conduct, which God forbid, the prioress or abbot should follow the procedure of a wise physician. After applying compresses, the ointment of encouragement, the medicine of divine scripture, and finally the cauterizing iron of excommunication and strokes of the rod, if they then perceive that their earnest efforts are unavailing, let them apply an even better remedy: they and all the members should pray for them so that God, who can do all things, may bring about the health of the sick one. Yet if even this procedure does not heal them, then finally, the prioress or abbot must use the knife and amputate. For the apostle says: 'Banish the evil one from your midst' (1 Corinthians 5:13); and again, 'If the unbeliever departs, let that one depart' (1 Corinthians 7:15), lest one diseased sheep infect the whole flock.

Reflection

In chapter 23, we considered the 'three strikes' approach to those who are at fault. Here, St Benedict provides an alternative, by drawing a parallel with the work of a physician treating a sick person.

First, apply the equivalent of a compress – trying some different 'light touch' ways of helping the person involved. If that doesn't work, then, second, use some 'ointment of encouragement' (and wouldn't we all benefit from someone applying such ointment to us each day?). Failing that, third, the medicine of divine scripture – using the Bible to both admonish and affirm. And then, if still no change, fourth, a symbolic cauterising of the 'infected part' – exclusion from the community and punishment. But even then, if the person still does not acknowledge or repent from their faults, the community still does not give up on them: fifth, they pray. And if that still doesn't work, then ultimately it can be the offender who through their response brings about their separation.

Choose one of the five methods described above and think about how you might apply this method in your own situation.

Read
Psalms 86—87

Pray
I pray for those I know to be in difficult situations.

·····†·····

6 Mar, 6 Jul, 5 Nov

Chapter 29: Readmission of members who leave the monastery

If any community members, following their own evil ways, leave the monastery but then wish to return, they must first promise to make full amends for leaving. Let them be received back, but as a test of humility they should be given the last place. If they leave again, or even a third time, they should be readmitted under the same conditions. After this, however, they must understand that they will be denied all prospect of return.

Reflection

The message from all that we have read over these last few days is that the way of unconditional love is not to give up on people. Even those who have so greatly offended us, if they seek to make amends, are to be welcomed back.

But it's also not practical to carry on as if nothing has happened – nor would it be wise to do so, in some cases. The frailties of the human condition are such that errant behaviour may well be repeated and, if we are to be realistic, that possibility has to be taken into account. To be blunt, this is unconditional love with conditions.

Think about a time when you felt repeatedly hurt. How has that influenced your approach to other people?

Read
Psalm 88

Pray
Lord, please heal my wounds.

7 Mar, 7 Jul, 6 Nov

Chapter 30: The manner of reproving the young

Every age and level of understanding should receive appropriate treatment. Therefore, as often as the young, or those who cannot understand the seriousness of the penalty of excommunication, are guilty of misdeeds, they should be subjected to severe fasts or checked with sharp strokes so that they may be healed.

Reflection

Joan Chittister asks if this chapter is still relevant for today: 'The real point of this and all seven preceding chapters of the penal code of the Rule is that Benedictine punishment is always meant to heal, never to destroy; to cure, not to crush.'[47]

The teaching we have been considering is also aimed at increasing stability. St Augustine of Hippo summarises this core principle well: 'And so love was present under the old covenant just as it is under the new, though then it was more hidden and fear was more apparent, whereas now love is more clearly seen and fear is diminished. For as love grows stronger we feel more secure, and when our feeling of security is complete fear vanishes, since, as the apostle John declares: Perfect love casts out fear (1 John 4:18).'[48]

As you reflect on the last few, somewhat difficult, chapters from the *Rule*, in what ways has it challenged your thinking about those who offend us or cause others difficulty?

Read
Psalm 89:1–18

Pray
Help me to love those who have caused harm.

8 Mar, 8 Jul, 7 Nov

Chapter 31: Qualifications of the monastery cellarer

As cellarer of the monastery, there should be chosen from the community someone who is wise, mature in conduct, temperate, not an excessive eater, not proud, excitable, offensive, dilatory or wasteful, but God-fearing, and like a parent to the whole community. The cellarer will take care of everything, but will do nothing without an order from the prioress or abbot. Let the cellarer keep to those orders.

The cellarer should not annoy the members. If anyone happens to make an unreasonable demand, the cellarer should not reject that person with disdain and cause distress, but reasonably and humbly deny the improper request. Let cellarers keep watch over their own souls, ever mindful of that saying of the apostle: 'They who serve well secure a good standing for themselves' (1 Timothy 3:13). The cellarer must show every care and concern for the sick, young, guests and the poor, knowing for certain that they will be held accountable for all of them on the day of judgment. The cellarer will regard all utensils and goods of the monastery as sacred vessels of the altar, aware that nothing is to be neglected. Cellarers should not be prone to greed, not be wasteful and extravagant with the goods of the monastery, but should do everything with moderation and according to the order of the prioress or abbot.

Reflection

Whether it's cups of tea, a Sunday roast or a healthy snack, the provision of food and drink is a significant, practical example of stability. Not only can we not live without it, but the very nature and routine of eating and drinking are an integral part of our health and well-being. By contrast, where that provision is lacking, stability is reduced. We only have to look at countries where there is famine or a lack of clean water to see the knock-on effects on individuals and society: those images of panic and near riot to collect food parcels from relief lorries, for example. We witness refugees fleeing war zones, stretching the resources of richer countries. But the apparently more prosperous societies are not exempt. In the UK, for example, the number of people given three-day emergency food supplies by food banks increased by 73% from 2014 to 2019, a stark example of increased instability in the lives of many people and families.[49]

Read
Psalm 89:19–37

Pray
I pray for those without adequate supplies of food and drink.

·····†·····

9 Mar, 9 Jul, 8 Nov

Chapter 31: Qualifications of the monastery cellarer

Above all, let the cellarer be humble. If goods are not available to meet a request, the cellarer will offer a kind word in reply, for it is written: 'A kind word is better than the best gift' (Sirach 18:17). Cellarers should take care of all that the prioress or abbot entrusts to them, and not presume to do what they have forbidden. They will provide the members their allotted amount of food without any pride or delay, lest they be led astray. For cellarers must remember what the scripture says that person deserves 'who leads one of the little ones astray' (Matthew 18:6).

If the community is rather large, the cellarer should be given helpers, that with their assistance they may calmly perform the duties of the office. Necessary items are to be requested and given at proper times, so that no one may be disquieted or distressed in the house of God.

Reflection

Following on from yesterday, those who provide such refreshment, such as a cellarer in a monastic community, a waiter in a restaurant or a parent cooking a meal for their family, also play a vital part in maintaining our human and spiritual stability. We can think about many others also: farmers growing crops and providing meat and dairy products; people working in processing and manufacturing and distribution, catering and retail outlets; chefs, bakers and homemakers.

Think about those who provide the food and drink that you consume.

Read
Psalm 89:38–52

Pray
I pray for those who put food and drink on our tables.

10 Mar, 10 Jul, 9 Nov

Chapter 32: The tools and goods of the monastery

The goods of the monastery, that is, its tools, clothing or anything else, should be entrusted to members whom the prioress or abbot appoints and in whose manner of life they have confidence. The abbot or prioress will, as they see fit, issue to them the various articles to be cared for and collected after use. The prioress and abbot will maintain a list of these, so that when the members succeed one another in their assigned tasks, they may be aware of what they hand out and what they receive back.

Whoever fails to keep the things belonging to the monastery clean or treats them carelessly should be reproved. If they do not amend, let them be subjected to the discipline of the Rule.

Reflection

The assignment of tools, clothing and equipment to workers has happened for centuries. People not only learn the 'tools of the trade' but actually own them – such as a chef with their own set of knives or a carpenter with their toolbox. Such items not only symbolise what a person does but are also part of their identity and how they relate to others: a doctor with a stethoscope or a vicar wearing a dog collar gives people confidence and trust in what they do.

In the same way that the cellarer regarded the kitchen utensils as sacred (see two days ago), so are all tools and equipment to be used with care and respect, for they are part of what is done in the practical Work of God alongside the prayerful Work of God.

What tools and equipment do you use at work, at home or in church? How do they link together your practical and your prayerful Work of God?

Read
Psalm 90

Pray
May the tools and equipment I use be instruments of prayer.

·····†·····

11 Mar, 11 Jul, 10 Nov

Chapter 33: Monastics and private ownership

Above all, this evil practice must be uprooted and removed from the monastery. We mean that without an order from the prioress or abbot, no members may presume to give, receive or retain anything as their own, nothing at all – not a book, writing tablets or stylus – in short not a single item, especially since monastics may not have the free disposal even of their own bodies and wills. For their needs, they are to look to the prioress or abbot of the monastery, and are not allowed anything which the prioress or abbot has not given or permitted. 'All things should be the common possession of all, as it is written, so that no one presumes ownership of anything' (Acts 4:32).

But if any members are caught indulging in this most evil practice, they should be warned a first and a second time. If they do not amend, let them be subjected to punishment.

Reflection

We may or may not live a community lifestyle where everything is shared. But imagine a life without any possessions, if we owned nothing. True enough, many people do not own their own home. Many have possessions for which they are still paying. But how about having no phone, no books, no tablet, no TV? (Don't worry, as we'll see later, St Benedict is fine about clothes, bedding and furniture!)

The fact is that our sense of stability is often dependent on our possessions. If we lack some 'basic essentials' of modern-day living or don't have what we need, then it can affect our health or make us feel insecure. In a different way, if our 'wants' (as distinct from our 'needs') are never satisfied, jealousy and frustration can eat away at our soul.

A message here for our 21st-century lives is not that having possessions is 'evil'; it's that if they were all stripped away, in what would the stability of our life and our faith be grounded?

Read
Psalm 91

Pray
May that which I own not be a barrier but a conduit towards knowing you more deeply.

12 Mar, 12 Jul, 11 Nov

Chapter 34: Distribution of goods according to need

It is written: 'Distribution was made as each had need' (Acts 4:35). By this we do not imply that there should be favouritism – God forbid – but rather consideration for weaknesses. Whoever needs less should thank God and not be distressed, but those who need more should feel humble because of their weakness, not self-important because of the kindness shown them. In this way all the members will be at peace. First and foremost, there must be no word or sign of the evil of grumbling, no manifestation of it for any reason at all. If, however, anyone is caught grumbling, let them undergo more severe discipline.

Reflection

In this chapter, St Benedict captures the concept of what we now call 'equality'. Equality is not about everyone being the same – indeed, it's not always about treating everyone in the same way either. Equality is about ensuring that every individual has an equal opportunity to make the most of their lives and talents and that no one should have poorer life-chances because of actual or perceived disadvantages.[50]

St Benedict even writes about what is described today as 'making reasonable adjustments' – not favouritism because of disadvantages, but making changes or providing ways in which any needs can be ameliorated to enable the achievement of someone's full potential as one beloved by God.

All this is connected to the concept of inclusion. Inclusion is not just about doing things to enable everyone to be included: it is also about giving people the ability to choose whether or not they wish to be included.

What thoughts and attitudes does this raise for you?

Read
Psalms 92—93

Pray
Help me, Lord, to be actively mindful of others.

·····✝·····

13 Mar, 13 Jul, 12 Nov

Chapter 35: Kitchen servers of the week

The members should serve one another. Consequently, no members will be excused from kitchen service unless they are sick or engaged in some important business of the monastery, for such service increases reward and fosters love. Let those who are not strong have help so that they may serve without distress, and let everyone receive help as the size of the community or local conditions warrant. If the community is rather large, the cellarer should be excused from kitchen service, and, as we have said, those should also be excused who are engaged in important business. Let all the rest serve one another in love.

On Saturday the ones who are completing their work will do the washing. They are to wash the towels which the members use to wipe their hands and feet. Both the one who is ending service and the one who is about to begin are to wash the feet of everyone. The utensils required for the kitchen service

**are to be washed and returned intact to the cellarer, who in
turn issues them to the one beginning the next week. In this
way the cellarer will know what is handed out and what is
received back.**

Reflection

This chapter considers two themes – the model of serving one
another (upon which we will reflect tomorrow) and the symbolism
of foot-washing.

You are probably familiar with the occasion during the last supper
when Jesus washed his disciples' feet. Take a few moments to read
John 13:1–17 and as you do so, sit quietly. Close your eyes or use a
focal point, such as a candle, to aid the stillness and openness to
listen to God.

Imagine you are in that room along with the disciples and others
who were gathered there. You hear the noise of conversation and
the rattle of utensils and pots. You smell the bread. You notice the
pouring of wine.

Now, read the passage again. Focus on a word, sentence or picture
that strikes you. What might God be saying to you?

Read
Psalm 94

Pray
Use the word, sentence or picture to listen to God and pray to him.

14 Mar, 14 Jul, 13 Nov

Chapter 35: Kitchen servers of the week

An hour before mealtime, the kitchen workers of the week should each receive a drink and some bread over and above the regular portion, so that at mealtime, they may serve one another without grumbling or hardship. On solemn days, however, they should wait until after the dismissal.

On Sunday immediately after Lauds, those beginning as well as those completing their week of service should make a profound bow in the oratory before all and ask for their prayers. Let the server completing the week recite this verse: 'Blessed are you, O God, who have helped me and comforted me' (Daniel 3:52;[51] Psalm 86:17). After this verse has been said three times the server receives a blessing. Then the one beginning the service follows and says: 'O God, come to my assistance; O God, make haste to help me' (Psalm 70:1). And all repeat this verse three times. When they have received a blessing, the servers begin their service.

Reflection

Yesterday reminded us of the fact that Jesus himself came not to be served but to serve.

Return now to the silent place where you were yesterday: the last supper. Sit with the disciples and others who were gathered there. Recall the same noises and the same smells. Bring to mind anything that God said to you in that time. Read John 13:1–17 again, if that would be helpful.

Imagine now Jesus coming towards you. He kneels before you. He washes your feet. He dries them with a towel.

What might he say? What look is in his face? What do you say in response?

Read
Psalms 95—96

Pray
Pray as God leads you.

......†......

15 Mar, 15 Jul, 14 Nov

Chapter 36: The sick

Care of the sick must rank above and before all else so that they may truly be served as Christ who said: 'I was sick and you visited me' (Matthew 25:36) and, 'What you did for one of these least of my people you did for me' (Matthew 25:40). Let the sick on their part bear in mind that they are served out of honour for God, and let them not by their excessive demands distress anyone who serves them. Still, the sick must be patiently borne with, because serving them leads to a greater reward. Consequently, the prioress or abbot should be extremely careful that they suffer no neglect.

Let a separate room be designated for the sick, and let them be served by an attendant who is God-fearing, attentive and concerned. The sick may take baths whenever it is advisable, but the healthy, and especially the young, should receive permission less readily. Moreover, to regain their strength, the sick who are very weak may eat meat, but when their health improves, they should all abstain from meat as usual.

The abbot and prioress must take the greatest care that cellarers and those who serve the sick do not neglect them for the shortcomings of disciples are their responsibility.

Reflection

Caring for those who are unwell or who live with a physical or mental health condition or a learning difference is of primary importance in any society. There are times when such caring, whether as a relative, friend, pastor or healthcare professional, comes at enormous personal, practical and financial cost. Thus, caring for the carers is also important.

But St Benedict picks up a less recognised issue: that of the responsibility of the person being cared for. Many people with such health conditions are, quite understandably, angry or bitter about the impact it has had upon them and their lifestyle. It's horrible when one cannot do the things one would like to do because the body or the mind will not allow it. Sadly, for some, the health condition becomes their identity – they define themselves by what they 'suffer' or are unable to do and not by who they are.

Read
Psalms 97—98

Pray
Lord, whatever happens, let me not forget the person I really am.

·····✝·····

16 Mar, 16 Jul, 15 Nov

Chapter 37: The elderly and the young

Although human nature itself is inclined to be compassionate toward the elderly and the young, the authority of the Rule should also provide for them. Since their lack of strength must always be taken into account, they should certainly not be required to follow the strictness of the Rule with regard to food, but should be treated with kindly consideration and allowed to eat before the regular hours.

Reflection

'There is a common belief that we gradually become less useful as we grow older,' writes Jada Pryor. 'That this world is made for the young. Perhaps that is so. But we are not of this world. When we live our lives for God, our journey here does not end until we take our final breath.'[52]

Jesus said, 'Let the little children come to me, and do not stop them; for it is to such as these that the kingdom of heaven belongs.'
MATTHEW 19:14 (see also MARK 10:14)

[Jesus] said, 'Truly I tell you, unless you change and become like children, you will never enter the kingdom of heaven. Whoever becomes humble like this child is the greatest in the kingdom of heaven. Whoever welcomes one such child in my name welcomes me.'
MATTHEW 18:3–5

So, what about in your church? Are children seen as a noisy distraction or the heartbeat of a joyful noise unto the Lord?

Even to your old age I am he, even when you turn grey I will carry you.

ISAIAH 46:4

Is wisdom with the aged, and understanding in length of days?

JOB 12:12

Do not speak harshly to an older man, but speak to him as to a father, to younger men as brothers, to older women as mothers, to younger women as sisters – with absolute purity.

1 TIMOTHY 5:1–2

And how about older people? Do you view them as 'blockers', who want things to be as they used to be, or are they honoured as wise guardians of the faith?

Read
Psalms 99—101

Pray
Help me to remember that aging is a process but 'old' is a state of mind.[53]

17 Mar, 17 Jul, 16 Nov

Chapter 38: The reader for the week

Reading will always accompany the meals. The reader should not be the one who just happens to pick up the book, but someone who will read for a whole week, beginning on Sunday. After Mass and Communion, let the incoming reader ask all to pray so that God may shield them from the spirit of vanity. Let the reader begin this verse in the oratory: 'O God, open my lips, and my mouth shall proclaim your praise' (Psalm 51:15), and let all say it three times. When they have received a blessing, they will begin their week of reading.

Let there be complete silence. No whispering, no speaking – only the reader's voice should be heard there. The members should by turn serve one another's needs as they eat and drink, so that no one need ask for anything. If, however, anything is required, it should be requested by an audible signal of some kind rather than by speech. No one should presume to ask a question about the reading or about anything else, 'lest occasions be given to the devil' (Ephesians 4:27; 1 Timothy 5:14). The abbot or prioress, however, may wish to say a few words of instruction.

Because of Communion and because the fast may be too hard for them to bear, the one who is reader for the week is to receive some diluted wine before beginning to read. Afterward they will take their meal with the weekly kitchen servers and the attendants.

Monastics will read and sing, not according to rank, but according to their ability to benefit their hearers.

Reflection

Although it takes a bit of getting used to, there is something quite special about eating a meal with other people in complete silence. Being silent allows time and space to be still, time to listen to the rattle of utensils and pots or to notice the smell of bread and the pouring of drink. It gives us space to give thanks for all those who grew, produced, distributed, cooked and served the food that sits in front of us: to give thanks to God for all that he provides.

The addition of a solo voice reading from the Bible or the *Rule* provides a further source on which to meditate and focus on listening to God.

While one wouldn't advocate this approach in family or other meal times when conversation is to be cherished and valued, you may like to try it on specific occasions.

Read
Psalm 102

Pray
May I listen to you through all my senses.

·····✝·····

18 Mar, 18 Jul, 17 Nov

Chapter 39: The proper amount of food

For the daily meals, whether at noon or in mid-afternoon, it is enough, we believe, to provide all the tables with two kinds of cooked food because of individual weaknesses. In this way, the person who may not be able to eat one kind of food may partake of the other. Two kinds of cooked food, therefore, should suffice for all, and if fruit or fresh vegetables are available, a third dish may also be added. A generous pound of bread is enough for a day whether for only one meal or for both dinner and supper. In the latter case the cellarer will set aside one third of this pound and give it to the community at supper.

Should it happen that the work is heavier than usual, the abbot and prioress may decide – and they will have the authority – to grant something additional, provided that it is appropriate, and that above all overindulgence is avoided, lest anyone experience indigestion. For nothing is so inconsistent with the life of any Christian as overindulgence. Our God says: 'Take care that your hearts are not weighted down with overindulgence' (Luke 21:34).

The young should not receive the same amount as their elders, but less, since in all matters frugality is the rule. Let everyone, except the sick who are very weak, abstain entirely from eating the meat of four-footed animals.

Reflection

In chapter 31, we reflected on the importance of food and mealtimes in maintaining our sense of stability. Food is the fuel we need to function. Yet, as humans, we often have a complex relationship with food which goes beyond simple likes and dislikes. For many, a health condition means the need to follow a particular, often restrictive diet, and meals can lose some of their enjoyment as a result. For some, the consumption of food is tightly entwined with mental well-being.

The routine of breakfast, lunch and dinner, however, is a useful parallel with approaches to prayer such as the Opus Dei. Breakfast can be a time when we place the day before the Lord; lunch an occasion to give thanks for what has taken place and to pray for the hours to come; and dinner to reflect on the Lord's presence throughout the day that has past. And there's always time for snacks… prayer can be devoured at any time!

In what ways might your mealtimes be symbols of your personal prayer?

Read
Psalm 103

Pray
Let me feed on your word and your presence, Lord.

19 Mar, 19 Jul, 18 Nov

Chapter 40: The proper amount of drink

'Everyone has personal gifts from God, one this and another that' (1 Corinthians 7:7). It is, therefore, with some uneasiness that we specify the amount of food and drink for others. However, with due regard for the infirmities of the sick, we believe that a half bottle of wine a day is sufficient for each. But those to whom God gives the strength to abstain must know that they will earn their own reward.

The abbot or prioress will determine when local conditions, work or the summer heat indicates the need for a greater amount. They must, in any case, take great care lest excess or drunkenness creep in. We read that monastics should not drink wine at all, but since the monastics of our day cannot be convinced of this, let us at least agree to drink moderately, and not to the point of excess, for 'wine makes even the wise go astray' (Sirach 19:2).

However, where local circumstances dictate an amount much less than what is stipulated above, or even none at all, those who live there should bless God and not grumble. Above all else we admonish them to refrain from grumbling.

Reflection

While giving half a bottle of wine to the sick would not be advocated today,[54] St Benedict acknowledges a need not to ban alcohol completely. The 'demon drink' has been the focus of campaigns and arguments for centuries, and alcohol can both bring people together and ruin lives; it can be a source of both pleasure and pain.

But the point of this chapter, as Norvene Vest observes, is to explore the nature of restraint in spiritual life: 'Sirach says: seek wisdom. Paul says: live by the Spirit. Benedict says: bless God. In Benedict's hands, all this advice on spiritual essentials has an earthy quality, a kind of fullness of delight in what actually is. How much I would like to live in a community where these constraints infused-with-glory provided the daily rhythm!'[55]

How is restraint an important factor in the stability of our faith?

Read
Psalm 104:1–26

Pray
Lord, grant me strength when needed in order that I might receive your rewards.

20 Mar, 20 Jul, 19 Nov

Chapter 41: The times for meals

From Easter to Pentecost, the monastics eat at noon and take supper in the evening. Beginning with Pentecost and continuing throughout the summer, the members fast until mid-afternoon on Wednesday and Friday, unless they are working in the fields or the summer heat is oppressive.

On the other days they eat dinner at noon. Indeed, the abbot or prioress may decide that they should continue to eat dinner at noon every day if they have work in the fields or if the summer heat remains extreme. Similarly, they should so regulate and arrange all matters that souls may be saved and the members may go about their activities without justifiable grumbling.

From the thirteenth of September to the beginning of Lent, they always take their meal in mid-afternoon. Finally, from the beginning of Lent to Easter, they eat towards evening. Let Vespers be celebrated early enough so that there is no need for a lamp while eating, and that everything can be finished by daylight. Indeed, at all times let supper or the hour of the fast-day meal be so scheduled that everything can be done by daylight.

Reflection

Routine, routine, routine. In some respects, the Benedictine approach could be viewed as a boring, unstimulating concept: doing the same thing, day after day, like a repetitive factory job or a church service that hasn't changed for generations.

And yet, we mustn't underestimate the value of routine. Indeed, routine is most often noticed when it's absent: in the loss of a job, for example. For people who go out to work, there is the daily routine of getting up, the journey to work, being with people, the regular tasks, the lunch break, the journey home. In a period of unemployment, sickness absence or retirement, the routine disappears. Loss of routine often leads to loss of confidence and contact with others.

As we've seen over these last few chapters, routine is an integral part of our stability, be that in the practicalities of meals or times of prayer. Such stable elements enable our faith to grow: stability leads to change.

In what ways does your routine help maintain your stability?

Read
Psalm 104:27–35

Pray
Help me, Lord, in the routine aspects of life, that they may enable me to grow and change.

····· † ·····

21 Mar, 21 Jul, 20 Nov

Chapter 42: Silence after Compline

> Monastics should diligently cultivate silence at all times, but especially at night. Accordingly, this will always be the arrangement whether for fast days or for ordinary days. When there are two meals, all will sit together immediately after rising from supper. Someone should read from the Conference[56] or the Lives[57] of the early Church writers or at

any rate something else that will benefit the hearers, but not the Heptateuch[58] or the Books of Kings, because it will not be good for those of weak understanding to hear these writings at that hour; they should be read at other times.

On fast days there is to be a short interval between Vespers and the reading of the Conferences, as we have indicated. Then let four or five pages be read, or as many as time permits. This reading period will allow for all to come together, in case any were engaged in assigned tasks. When all have assembled, they should pray Compline; and on leaving Compline, no one will be permitted to speak further. If monastics are found to transgress this rule of silence, they must be subjected to severe punishment, except on occasions when guests require attention or the prioress or abbot wishes to give someone a command, but even this is to be done with the utmost seriousness and proper restraint.

Reflection

In a monastic community, day moves into night with The Great Silence. Esther de Waal writes how this is a 'deep interior silence which is such a creative part of life, of any life, since it allows us to hear the Word of God in the depths of our hearts and to rest there through the hours of darkness'.[59]

Silence frees us from some of the distractions of everyday life and allows us to listen and to give intentional attention to God. And yet, be it at night or in the day, being silent doesn't automatically mean that God will speak. It's easy to think, 'Right, your turn now, God.' We sit in silence, wanting to hear God's voice: 'Speak, for your servant is listening' (1 Samuel 3:10). And we may well hear it but God also 'speaks through the earthquake, wind and fire',[60] the noise that surrounds us and inhabits our very being.

'Our words are too fragile. God's silence is too deep,' as Barbara Brown Taylor puts it. 'Silence is as much a sign of God's presence as of God's absence – divine silence is not a vacuum to be filled but a mystery to be entered into.'[61]

In what ways do you hear God's voice?

Read
Psalm 105:1–22

Pray
Thank you, God, that you listen to me when I wish to speak. May I listen when you to speak to me.

·····✝·····

22 Mar, 22 Jul, 21 Nov

Chapter 43: Tardiness at the Opus Dei or at table

On hearing the signal for an hour of the divine office, monastics will immediately set aside what they have in hand and go with utmost speed, yet with gravity and without giving occasion for frivolity. Indeed, nothing is to be preferred to the Opus Dei.

If at Vigils monastics come after the Doxology of Psalm 94, which we wish, therefore, to be said quite deliberately and slowly, they are not to stand in their regular place in choir. They must take the last place of all, or one set apart by the prioress or abbot for such offenders, that they may be seen by them and by all, until they do penance by public satisfaction at the end of the Opus Dei. We have decided, therefore, that they ought to stand either in the last place or apart from the others so that the attention they attract will shame them into amending. Should they remain outside the oratory, there may be those who would return to bed and sleep, or, worse yet, settle down outside and engage in idle talk, thereby 'giving occasion to the Evil One' (Ephesians 4:27; 1 Timothy 5:14). They should come inside so that they will not lose everything and may amend in the future.

At the day hours the same rule applies to those who come after the opening verse and the Doxology of the first Psalm following it: They are to stand in the last place. Until they have made satisfaction, they are not to presume to join the choir of those praying the Psalms, unless perhaps the prioress or abbot pardons them and grants an exception. Even in this case, the one at fault is still bound to satisfaction.

Reflection

Nothing is to be preferred to the Work of God. Whatever we are doing: stop. No matter how busy we are or think we ought to be: stop. Regardless of how important or mundane the task: stop. Nothing is to be preferred to the Work of God.

'Prayer helps us to have the strength to deal with what we will face when we get up from our knees.'[62] If we are to learn anything from our reflections on the *Rule of St Benedict*, it is that prayer and praise take priority. Alongside our 'I've just got to do…' delaying tactics, there are genuine, unavoidable and important events that detract us at times. Sometimes our own personal Opus Dei might have to be done differently as a result. The discipline and the routine do take practice – and the benefits are enormous. It's putting aside time to give God intentional attention. It's like having an appointment, and a day without one feels less complete.

The Work of God provides stability, enables us to listen and, over time, changes who we are.

How is your own Opus Dei taking shape?

Read
Psalm 105:23–45

Pray
Lord, help me to give my intentional attention to you.

23 Mar, 23 Jul, 22 Nov

Chapter 43: Tardiness at the Opus Dei or at table

But, if monastics do not come to table before the verse so that all may say the verse and pray and sit down at table together, and if this failure happens through their own negligence or fault, they should be reproved up to the second time. If they still do not amend, let them not be permitted to share the common table, but take their meals alone, separated from the company of all. Their portion of wine should be taken away until there is satisfaction and amendment. Anyone not present for the verse said after meals is to be treated in the same manner.

No one is to presume to eat or drink before or after the time appointed. Moreover, if anyone is offered something by the prioress or abbot and refuses it, then, if the monastic later wants what was refused or anything else, that one should receive nothing at all until appropriate amends have been made.

Reflection

Over the last few chapters, we've reflected on the importance of food and mealtimes from both the physical and spiritual health-giving aspects. This is all part of the 'whole-life balance' touched upon right back in chapter 4. So our physical needs are to be sustained by putting aside time for meals and our spiritual needs are to be sustained by similar commitments. All these, as we have already considered, are important for stability in life and faith.

Esther de Waal reflects on the security that comes from living in the knowledge that here is a right time and right place for eating and for praying: 'Respecting boundaries, not letting things drift, means that I am totally present to whatever I am doing, present with awareness, and therefore with energy for whatever that place, that moment may bring me.'[63]

You may like to develop your own personal 'Rule of Life' (see an example of one on page 199).

Read
Psalm 106:1–12

Pray
I give my whole life to you.

24 Mar, 24 Jul, 23 Nov

Chapter 44: Satisfaction by the excommunicate

Those excommunicated for serious faults from the oratory and from the table are to prostrate themselves in silence at the oratory entrance at the end of the celebration of the Opus Dei. They should lie face down at the feet of all as they leave the oratory, and let them do this until the prioress or abbot judges they have made satisfaction. Next, at the bidding of the prioress or abbot, they are to prostrate themselves at the feet of the prioress or abbot, then at the feet of all that they may pray for them. Only then, if the prioress or abbot orders, should they be admitted to the choir in the rank the prioress or abbot assigns. Even so, they should not presume to lead a Psalm or a reading or anything else in the oratory without further instructions from the prioress or abbot. In addition, at all the hours, as the Opus Dei is being completed, they must prostrate themselves in the place they occupy. They will continue this form of satisfaction until the prioress or abbot again bids them cease.

Those excommunicated for less serious faults from the table only are to make satisfaction in the oratory for as long as the prioress or abbot orders. They do so until they give them blessing and say: 'Enough.'

Reflection

The letter had meant well. It was written from the heart. I asked for forgiveness. It offered forgiveness. It was met with anger.

Those who have wronged us are sometimes, deep down inside, never truly forgiven. Anger, hurt and bitterness can be carried for years. We can ruminate about what happened over and over again, blaming other people, blaming ourselves, blaming God.

Paul's letter to Galatians highlights the cost: 'If, however, you bite and devour one another, take care that you are not consumed by one another' (Galatians 5:15).

How long does it have to be and what does it take to say, 'Enough'?

Read
Psalm 106:13–33

Pray
Forgive us our sins as we forgive those who sin against us.

25 Mar, 25 Jul, 24 Nov

Chapter 45: Mistakes in the oratory

Should monastics make a mistake in a Psalm, responsory, refrain or reading, they must make satisfaction there before all. If they do not use this occasion to humble themselves, they will be subjected to more severe punishment for failing to correct by humility the wrong committed through negligence. Youth, however, are to be whipped for such a fault.

Reflection

We all make mistakes. It's what we do with them that counts.

So many times, a mistake can grow into something much bigger than was either anticipated or desired. Things get out of hand. At their worst, the consequences of some mistakes can feel like 'being whipped'.

St Benedict advocates a prompt acknowledgement and apology as the most effective response. We are to 'use this occasion', the very moment the mistake takes place, to show such humility.

Why do we find it hard to admit mistakes?

Read
Psalm 106:34–48

Pray
Help me not to be ashamed about admitting my mistakes.

·····✝·····

26 Mar, 26 Jul, 25 Nov

Chapter 46: Faults committed in other matters

If monastics commit a fault while at any work – while working in the kitchen, in the storeroom, in serving, in the bakery, in the garden, in any craft of anywhere else – either by breaking or losing something or failing in any other way in any other place, they must at once come before the prioress or abbot and community and of their own accord admit their fault and make satisfaction. If it is made known through another, they are to be subjected to a more severe correction.

When the cause of the sin lies hidden in the conscience, the monastic is to reveal it only to the prioress or abbot or to one of the spiritual elders, who know how to heal their own wounds as well as those of others, without exposing them and making them public.

Reflection

Continuing the theme from yesterday, the need to acknowledge a mistake straight away goes against much of what we might have learnt as we grew up. School days were sometimes full of children threatening 'to tell the teacher' (or the school bully) if we did something wrong. Or, later in life, if we made a mistake at work or elsewhere, it may have taken more effort trying to cover it up than it did to simply admit to it. And to further complicate matters, owning up to a mistake also depends on the level of trust we have in the person we're telling.

What's been your experience? What worked and what didn't?

Read
Psalm 107:1–22

Pray
Give me the courage to admit to my mistakes.

27 Mar, 27 Jul, 26 Nov

Chapter 47: Announcing the hours for the Opus Dei

It is the responsibility of the abbot and prioress to announce, day and night, the hour for the Opus Dei. They may do so personally or delegate the responsibility to a conscientious member, so that everything may be done at the proper time.

Only those so authorised are to lead Psalms and refrains, after the prioress or abbot according to their rank. No monastics should presume to read or sing unless they are able to benefit the hearers; let this be done with humility, seriousness and reverence, and at the bidding of the prioress or abbot.

Reflection

Throughout the centuries, the church, the people of God, have come together to pray, to worship and to learn. Whether it's reading a passage from the Bible or leading the intercessions, singing in the choir or playing music, taking the service or preaching, taking part in building up the faith of the people of God is both a responsibility and a privilege.

Those who lead are to show those key facets of humility we considered in chapter 7 and elsewhere. They are to work with the agreement, approval and authority of others and to do so in a way which is reverent and enriching. There is also a need to be mindful of when worship, liturgy, sermon, choir, processions, music, etc. becomes a performance and diminishes our reverence for God the Father, God the Son and God the Holy Spirit.

In what ways is there a danger that we become so good at 'doing church' that we are not as good at 'doing God'?

Read
Psalm 107:23–43

Pray
May all our praise and prayer be of a pure heart.

·····†·····

28 Mar, 28 Jul, 27 Nov

Chapter 48: The daily manual labour

Idleness is the enemy of the soul. Therefore, the community members should have specified periods for manual labour as well as for prayerful reading.

We believe that the times for both may be arranged as follows: From Easter to the first of October, they will spend their mornings after Prime till about the fourth hour at whatever work needs to be done. From the fourth hour until the time of Sext, they will devote themselves to reading. But after Sext and their meal, they may rest on their beds in complete silence; should any members wish to read privately, let them do so, but without disturbing the others. They should say None a little early, about midway through the eighth hour, and then until Vespers they are to return to whatever work is necessary. They must not become distressed if local conditions or their poverty should force them to do the harvesting themselves. When they live by the labour of their hands, as our ancestors and the apostles did, then they are really monastics. Yet, all things are to be done with moderation on account of the fainthearted.

Reflection

'Superheroes don't work 90-hour weeks.'[64] Today's workplaces are very different to those of 30–40 years ago. In some, the focus is on speed not substance, quantity not quality and money not matter. For many workers, lunch breaks (let alone tea breaks) are a thing of the past. The advent of apps, smartphones and email have many benefits but have also created an 'always on' culture.

While the evidence clearly shows that good work is good for us[65] and enhances our stability and identity, it can at the same time have a damaging effect. Consider also the lives of those who are not in employment or are unable to work for health, family or other reasons. Far from choosing to be idle, such enforced inactivity diminishes self-worth and personhood. Overwork and inactivity can both be enemies of the soul.

Whether work-related or not, what might be described as your 'enemies of the soul': those factors which diminish your identity?

Read
Psalm 108

Pray
Thank you, Lord, that my true identity is in you.

29 Mar, 29 Jul, 28 Nov

Chapter 48: The daily manual labour

From the first of October to the beginning of Lent, the members ought to devote themselves to reading until the end of the second hour. At this time Terce is said and they are to work at their assigned tasks until None. At the first signal for the hour of None, all put aside their work to be ready for the second signal. Then after their meal they will devote themselves to their reading or to the Psalms.

During the days of Lent, they should be free in the morning to read until the third hour, after which they will work at their assigned tasks until the end of the tenth hour. During this time of Lent each one is to receive a book from the library and is to read the whole of it straight through. These books are to be distributed at the beginning of Lent.

Above all, one or two elders must surely be deputed to make the rounds of the monastery while the members are reading. Their duty is to see that no one is so apathetic as to waste time or engage in idle talk to the neglect of their reading, and so not only harm themselves but also distract others. If such persons are found – God forbid – they should be reproved a first and a second time. If they do not amend, they must be subjected to the punishment of the Rule as a warning to others. Further, members ought not to associate with one another at inappropriate times.

Reflection

The need for whole-life balance presents itself again. Time for work and time for prayerful reading, writes St Benedict. Whether it's reading or other restorative and beneficial activities, it's the setting aside that matters. Over the last few weeks, we've seen the value of setting aside time to give intentional attention to God. So too is it important to address those enemies of the soul and maintain the whole-life balance. True, there may be some aspects of life that we can't control, but we do have a choice as to how we respond.

How could your choices and responses help to improve whole-life balance?

Read
Psalm 109

Pray
Help me to make the right choices and responses.

·····†·····

30 Mar, 30 Jul, 29 Nov

Chapter 48: The daily manual labour

On Sunday all are to be engaged in reading except those who have been assigned various duties. If any are so remiss and indolent that they are unwilling or unable to study or to read, they are to be given some work in order that they may not be idle.

Those who are sick or weak should be given a type of work or craft that will keep them busy without overwhelming them or driving them away. The prioress or abbot must take their infirmities into account.

Reflection

Finding sabbath moments is, as we have already reflected upon, vital to tackling the enemies of the soul and maintaining whole-life balance. This chapter and the reflections upon it may have been quite challenging. If you are struggling to know what you can do to restore the balance, then one well-recognised, very practical approach can be helpful. Have a think about the following five areas of your life – it's been recognised that these are key to personal well-being and if one area is unfulfilled then our well-being is not as good:

- Connect – with other people around you.
- Be active – some form of physical exercise (don't automatically think 'gym': do what you enjoy and can manage).
- Take notice – of the beauty of creation and of what's happening for other people.
- Keep learning – a hobby, a course, reading: we can indeed learn something new every day.
- Give – to others, whether that's in church, at work, in family life, by volunteering or by simple, but often very powerful, random acts of kindness.

What do you do at the moment that relates to each of those 'Five Ways to Wellbeing'?[66]

What else could you do?

Read
Psalms 110—111

Pray
Thank you, Lord, that you care about the whole of my life.

·····†·····

31 Mar, 31 Jul, 30 Nov

Chapter 49: The observance of Lent

The life of a monastic ought to be a continuous Lent. Since few, however, have the strength for this, we urge the entire community during these days of Lent to keep its manner of life most pure and to wash away in this holy season the negligences of other times. This we can do in a fitting manner by refusing to indulge evil habits and by devoting ourselves to prayer with tears, to reading, to compunction of heart and self-denial. During these days, therefore, we will add to the usual measure of our service something by way of private prayer and abstinence from food or drink, so that each of us will have something above the assigned measure to offer God of our own will with the joy of the Holy Spirit (1 Thessalonians 1:6). In other words, let each one deny themselves some food, drink, sleep, needless talking and idle jesting, and look forward to holy Easter with joy and spiritual longing.

All should, however, make known to the prioress or abbot what they intend to do, since it ought to be done with their prayer and approval. Whatever is undertaken without the permission of the prioress or abbot will be reckoned as presumption and vainglory, not deserving a reward. Therefore, everything must be done with their approval.

Reflection

'The life of a monastic ought to be a continuous Lent… and look forward to holy Easter with joy and spiritual longing.' Thomas Kardong OSB writes, 'If I had to pick out one of Benedict's pithy sayings to take along to a desert island, I think this is one I could not do without.'[67]

While Lent is sometimes thought of as a time for self-denial, it is also a specific period to focus on change and growth. If you're reading this at the end of March, then you might well still be in Lent. If it's July or November, then maybe, as you have made this journey with St Benedict, life has taken on a sense of continuous Lent. You may be in a time of change and growth or a period of listening more to God and increased stability. You may have noticed an inner change of looking forward with joy and spiritual longing.

Write down three things which provide you with a deeper sense of joy and spiritual longing.

Read
Psalms 112—113

Pray
May I always be looking forward with joy and spiritual longing.

·····✝·····

1 Apr, 1 Aug, 1 Dec

Chapter 50: Members working at a distance or travelling

Members who work so far away that they cannot return to the oratory at the proper time – and the prioress or abbot determines that is the case – are to perform the Opus Dei where they are, and kneel out of reverence for God.

So too, those who have been sent on a journey are not to omit the prescribed hours but to observe them as best they can, not neglecting their measure of service.

Reflection

It had been a year of enormous change and a time of instability, but a routine work trip provided an unexpected way forward. The hotel room was quiet, and reading Jesus' encounter with Bartimaeus was familiar and comfortable (Mark 10:46–52).

'What do you want me to do for you?'

My eyes opened wide as the words leapt off the page. Who, me? Jesus, asking me? It was as if I had regained my sight. After years of living in a spiritual desert, I knew what I wanted Jesus to do. It would be days before I could even begin to tell him but, over the next few months, I followed Jesus to a deeper, more stable place.

Whether through work or on holiday, being away from home, and away from all the security that provides, can either detract from or deepen our intentional attention to God. Unfamiliar surroundings affect our routine but can also take away the unconscious and conscious distractions of home, allowing us to open our eyes to a new experience.

What do you want Jesus to do for you?

Read
Psalms 114—115

Pray
Lord Jesus, let my eyes be opened so I may see you more clearly.

2 Apr, 2 Aug, 2 Dec

Chapter 51: Members on a short journey

If members are sent on some errand and expect to return to the monastery that same day, they must not presume to eat outside, even if they receive a pressing invitation, unless perhaps the prioress or abbot has ordered it. Should they act otherwise, they will be excommunicated.

Reflection

As we've seen, for the monastic, meal times take on a sacramental quality and being in the community at such times is integral to their way of life. With his warning not to eat outside the community, St Benedict is alerting members to the distractions and difficulties that can exist in the world beyond the monastic enclosure.

Joan Chittister writes, 'Benedictine spirituality, this chapter implies, is not a set of rules; it is a way of life. Being out of the monastery does not relieve the monastic of the obligation to be what we say we are – simple, centred in God, in search of higher things.'[68]

What aspects of life detract or interfere with the desire to listen to God, to be open to change and to enable stability?

Read
Psalms 116—117

Pray
As I see you more clearly, Lord, may I remain focused on you.

3 Apr, 3 Aug, 3 Dec

Chapter 52: The oratory of the monastery

The oratory ought to be what it is called, and nothing else is to be done or stored there. After the Opus Dei, all should leave in complete silence and with reverence for God, so that anyone who may wish to pray alone will not be disturbed by the insensitivity of another. Moreover, if at other times some choose to pray privately, they may simply go in and pray, not in a loud voice, but with tears and heartfelt devotion. Accordingly, those who do not pray in this manner are not to remain in the oratory after the Opus Dei, as we have said; then they will not interfere with anyone else.

Reflection

Meaning 'a place of prayer', the oratory is set aside solely for giving intentional attention to God.

While we might grab a few head-bowed moments in the pew, today's church services are, quite rightly, preceded and followed by conversation, thus silence may not be something easily acquired on the average Sunday.

It is perhaps at home, therefore, that we can most effectively create our own place of prayer. It may be in the corner of a room; a place that is free from distraction (not sharing a desk with a computer, for example); a place distinguished by a small table, prayer stool, icon or candle: a place whose sole purpose is one of prayer.

What might your oratory look like?

Read
Psalm 118

Pray
May my place of prayer be a place to meet with you.

4 Apr, 4 Aug, 4 Dec

Chapter 53: The reception of guests

All guests who present themselves are to be welcomed as Christ, who said: 'I was a stranger and you welcomed me' (Matthew 25:35). Proper honour must be shown 'to all, especially to those who share our faith' (Galatians 6:10) and to pilgrims.

Once guests have been announced, the prioress or abbot and the community are to meet them with all the courtesy of love. First of all, they are to pray together and thus be united in peace, but prayer must always precede the kiss of peace because of the delusions of the devil.

All humility should be shown in addressing a guest on arrival or departure. By a bow of the head or by a complete prostration of the body, Christ is to be adored and welcomed in them. After the guests have been received, they should be invited to pray; then the abbot or prioress or an appointed member will sit with them. The divine law is read to all guests for their instruction, and after that every kindness is shown to them. The prioress or abbot may break their fast for the sake of a guest, unless it is a day of special fast which cannot be broken. The members, however, observe the usual fast.

The abbot or prioress shall pour water on the hands of the guest, and the abbot or prioress with the entire community shall wash their feet. After washing they will recite this verse: 'God, we have received your mercy in the midst of your temple' (Psalm 48:9).

Great care and concern are to be shown in receiving poor people and pilgrims, because in them more particularly Christ is received; our very awe of the rich guarantees them special respect.

Reflection

Imagine for a moment:

- Treating every visitor to your home as if they were Christ.
- Serving every customer in your workplace as if they were Christ.
- Welcoming every person to your church as if they were Christ.

'Did we see Christ in them? Did they see Christ in us?' asks Esther de Waal. 'If we are really to receive everyone as Christ that means we must respect each as made in the image of God and not in the image of ourselves.'[69] For 'Christ is to be adored and welcomed in them'.

Read
Psalm 119:1–32

Pray
May I look for Christ in all people.

5 Apr, 5 Aug, 5 Dec

Chapter 53: The reception of guests

The kitchen for the abbot and prioress and guests ought to be separate, so that guests – and monasteries are never without them – need not disturb the community when they present themselves at unpredictable hours. Each year, two monastics who can do the work competently are to be assigned to this kitchen. Additional help should be available when needed, so that they can perform this service without grumbling. On the other hand, when the work slackens, they are to go wherever other duties are assigned them. This consideration is not for them alone, but applies to all duties in the monastery; members are to be given help when it is needed, and whenever they are free, they work wherever they are assigned.

The guest quarters are to be entrusted to a God-fearing member. Adequate bedding should be available there. The house of God should be in the care of members who will manage it wisely.

No monastics are to speak or associate with guests unless they are bidden; however, if the members meet or see guests, they are to greet them humbly, as we have said. They ask for a blessing and continue on their way, explaining that they are not allowed to speak.

Reflection

If we greet other people as if they were Christ, then our role as the one who welcomes them takes on a whole new meaning. Whether it's through the complexities of work, home or church, the making of a cup of tea or providing a bed for the night, as Christ-welcomers everything we do becomes an expression of God's love for another person. The ordinary and the everyday become extraordinary and eternal. For 'Christ is to be adored and welcomed in them'.

How does this influence your attitude towards other people?

Read
Psalm 119:33–56

Pray
May I look for Christ in all people.

·····†·····

6 Apr, 6 Aug, 6 Dec

Chapter 54: Letters or gifts

In no circumstance are monastics allowed, unless the prioress or abbot says they may, to exchange letters, blessed tokens or small gifts of any kind, with their parents or anyone else, or with another monastic. They must not presume to accept gifts sent them even by their parents without previously telling the prioress or abbot. If the prioress or abbot orders acceptance, they still have the power to give the gift to whomever; and the one for whom it was originally sent must not be distressed, 'lest occasion be given to the devil' (Ephesians 4:27; 1 Timothy 5:14). Whoever presumes to act otherwise will be subjected to the discipline of the Rule.

Reflection

Not for the first time, the austerity of the monastic lifestyle is striking. It is life stripped back to its bare essentials: anything (such as gifts or letters) that might possibly cause pride to be puffed up or jealousy to be created is forbidden.

At times such as Christmas and birthdays, presents can sometimes cause excitement and disappointment in equal measure. And then there are those unexpected tokens of appreciation – that card, that bunch of flowers – which can be so precious.

And yet such gratitude is often not given. It's a sad fact of working life that for many people, the only way they know they're doing a good job is because they're not being criticised: 'If no one says anything, I must be doing okay!' When was the last time someone thanked you or praised you for a piece of good work? Do you thank and praise your colleagues?

It's good and affirming to be thanked and praised for what we do and for the person we are. But the message goes even deeper than that. God knows all that we do, and our reward, the deepest thanks and praise, comes from him. As Jesus himself tells us, all that we do and all that we give is to 'be done in secret; and your Father who sees in secret will reward you' (Matthew 6:4).

Reflect on the concept of knowing it is sufficient that God sees what you do.

Read
Psalm 119:57–80

Pray
Thank you, Lord, that you know all I do. May all I do be for you.

······†······

7 Apr, 7 Aug, 7 Dec

Chapter 55: Clothing and footwear

The clothing distributed to the members should vary according to local conditions and climate, because more is needed in cold regions and less in warmer. This is left to the discretion of the prioress or abbot. We believe that for each monastic a cowl and tunic will suffice in temperate regions; in winter a woollen cowl is necessary, in summer a thinner or worn one; also a scapular for work, and footwear – both sandals and shoes.

Monastics must not complain about the colour or coarseness of all these articles, but use what is available in the vicinity at a reasonable cost. However, the prioress and abbot ought to be concerned about the measurements of these garments that they not be too short but fitted to the wearers.

Whenever new clothing is received, the old should be returned at once and stored in a wardrobe for the poor. To provide for laundering and night wear, every member will need two cowls and two tunics, but anything more must be taken away as superfluous. When new articles are received, the worn ones – sandals or anything old – must be returned.

Those going on a journey should get underclothing from the wardrobe. On their return they are to wash it and give it back. Their cowls and tunics, too, ought to be somewhat better than those they ordinarily wear. Let them get these from the wardrobe before departing, and on returning put them back.

Reflection

Whether it's a penchant for hats, shoes or jackets, the clothes we wear are often another expression of our stability. They can make us feel comfortable and confident. Whether fashionable or not, clothes can be part of who are we are as a person and who God calls us to be. And whether we have the security of an outfit for every possible occasion or are happy to pass some on to a charity shop, the *Rule* challenges our priorities; the repeated theme of where our stability finds its foundation arises once more.

In what ways does your clothing enhance your life of prayer?

Read
Psalm 119:81–104

Pray
Thank you, Lord, that you love both my outer and inner appearances.

8 Apr, 8 Aug, 8 Dec

Chapter 55: Clothing and footwear

For bedding monastics will need a mat, a woollen blanket and a light covering as well as a pillow.

The beds are to be inspected frequently by the prioress or abbot, lest private possessions be found there. Anyone discovered with anything not given by the prioress or abbot must be subjected to very severe punishment. In order that this vice of private ownership may be completely uprooted, the prioress or abbot is to provide all things necessary: that is, cowl, tunic, sandals, shoes, belt, knife, stylus, needle, handkerchief and writing tablets. In this way every excuse of lacking some necessity will be taken away.

The abbot and prioress, however, must always bear in mind what is said in the Acts of the Apostles: 'Distribution was made as each had need' (Acts 4:35). In this way the prioress and abbot will take into account the weakness of the needy, not the evil will of the envious: yet in all their judgments they must bear in mind God's retribution.

Reflection

Picking up yesterday's themes and those of the earlier parts of the *Rule*, such as chapter 33, we are reminded once again that our stability finds its foundations not in what we have or want but in what is absolutely necessary. And so it is that in this Benedictine world of minimalism and austerity, the *Rule* advocates one comfort that has remained unchanged in all these years: the bed. A mattress, a cover and a pillow.

Perhaps St Benedict knows what he's talking about, after all. The practicality and the spirituality of our stability requires that fundamental need for good sleep to be fulfilled. As we considered in chapter 22, without good sleep, we don't function as well. Disrupted sleep is often an outward sign of inner difficulty and discontent. Yet it's also unrealistic to expect to get 'a good eight hours' every single night – even if that would be nice! Sleep is another element not only of our stability but of the thread of whole-life balance which runs through our exploration of the *Rule*.

So, thinking back over the past five weeks or so since reflecting on this same topic, how's your sleep now? Does anything else need to be done to improve it?

Read
Psalm 119:105–128

Pray
May I lie down and sleep in peace, for you alone, Lord, make me dwell in safety (from Psalm 4:8).

9 Apr, 9 Aug, 9 Dec

Chapter 56: The prioress' or abbot's table

> The table of the prioress or abbot must always be with guests and travellers. Whenever there are no guests, it is within their right to invite anyone of the community they wish. However, for the sake of maintaining discipline, one or two seniors must always be left with the others.

Reflection

'The greater point of the chapter for us today is not the geography of the table but the fact that the leader of the community was expected to model the gift of self with strangers,' writes Joan Chittister. 'Hospitality in the Benedictine community was attention and presence to the needs of the other. Hospitality was a public ministry designed to nourish the other in body and in soul, in spirit and in psyche.'[70]

The gift of hospitality is one which reaches out not just to those we know but to those who are newcomers and visitors. Whether it's an invitation to Sunday lunch after church or a cup of tea at the local cafe, showing hospitality to others is a tangible demonstration of our care for others. It's not about the food and the drink; it's about the love, care and respect that those actions represent. After all, Christ's love shown through bread and wine carries much the same message.

Consider the role hospitality has played in your life and how it has demonstrated Christ's love for you and others.

Read
Psalm 119:129–152

Pray
Loving Lord, may the gifts of bread and wine be symbols of your love for all people.

10 Apr, 10 Aug, 10 Dec

Chapter 57: The artisans of the monastery

If there are artisans in the monastery, they are to practice their craft with all humility, but only with the permission of the prioress or the abbot. If one of them becomes puffed up by skilfulness in the craft, and feels that they are conferring something on the monastery, they are to be removed from practicing the craft and not allowed to resume it unless, after manifesting humility, they are so ordered by the prioress or abbot.

Whenever products of these artisans are sold, those responsible for the sale must not dare to practice any fraud. Let them always remember Ananias and Sapphira, who incurred bodily death (Acts 5:1–11), lest they and all who perpetrate fraud in monastery affairs suffer spiritual death.

The evil of avarice must have no part in establishing prices, which should, therefore, always be a little lower than people outside the monastery are able to set, 'so that in all things God may be glorified' (1 Peter 4:11).

Reflection

Our God is a creative God. One only needs to look at the countryside and its creatures, the skies and the seas to be reminded of God the artisan. Made in God's image, we too are blessed with creative ability. Some more than others? Well, maybe. It's not about it being good enough for others to marvel at, nor for excessive financial gain. Whether it's a craft, painting, drawing, music, writing, acting, photography, textiles, gardening or baking, our creative ability is a gift from God and one through which we can give glory to God.

If your creative thread is undiscovered or unfulfilled due to other commitments or perceived lack of ability, perhaps there is time to find something else which makes you you and contributes towards the person God wants you to be.

- What are your creative skills?
- In what ways do they give glory to God?
- What is it about them that helps make you the person you are?
- What would you like to develop further?

Read
Psalm 119:153–176

Pray
'All things come from you, and of your own have we given you' (1 Chronicles 29:14).

11 Apr, 11 Aug, 11 Dec

Chapter 58: The procedure for receiving members

Do not grant newcomers to the monastic life an easy entry, but, as the apostle says, 'Test the spirits to see if they are from God' (1 John 4:1). Therefore, if someone comes and keeps knocking at the door, and if at the end of four or five days has shown patience in bearing harsh treatment and difficulty of entry, and has persisted in the request, then that one should be allowed to enter and stay in the guest quarters for a few days. After that, the person should live in the novitiate, where the novices study, eat and sleep.

A senior chosen for skill in winning souls should be appointed to look after the newcomer with careful attention. The concern must be whether the novice truly seeks God and shows eagerness for the Opus Dei, for obedience and for trials. The novices should be clearly told all the hardships and difficulties that will lead to God.

If they promise perseverance in stability, then after two months have elapsed let this Rule be read straight through to them, and let them be told: 'This is the law under which you are choosing to serve. If you can keep it, come in. If not, feel free to leave.' If they still stand firm, they are to be taken back to the novitiate, and again thoroughly tested in all patience. After six months have passed, the Rule is to be read to them, so that they may know what they are entering. If once more they stand firm, let four months go by, and then read this Rule to them again. If after due reflection they promise to observe everything and to obey every command given them, let them then be received into the community. But they must be well aware that, as the law of the Rule establishes, from this day they are no longer free to leave the monastery, nor to shake from their neck the yoke of the Rule which, in the course of so prolonged a period of reflection, they were free either to reject or to accept.

Reflection

Discernment of God's calling often takes a while, whether it's to a particular job or making other big decisions such as moving to a new home. Something we hoped may have an immediate answer stretches into months. Questions such as 'Is this God's will – or mine?' dominate our thoughts and prayers. In times of confusion and uncertainty, we weigh up the pros and cons. We seek out those who affirm our view – but we also need those who through their careful attention will test it. Such prolonged periods of reflection are as much a part of discernment as the object of the calling itself. God gives us times of waiting for a reason.

Timothy Bavin OSB said, 'God calls us even if we don't realise it or we are unworthy of it. It is he who creates, enables and gives grace – it is his call. Our choice is to respond and in his great love and mercy, he also grants us the freedom to refuse.' [71]

What might God be calling you to do?

Read
Psalms 120—121

Pray
Lord, help me to listen to your calling and help me to respond.

12 Apr, 12 Aug, 12 Dec

Chapter 58: The procedure for receiving members

When they are to be received, they come before the whole community in the oratory and promise stability, fidelity to the monastic life, and obedience. This is done in the presence of God and the saints to impress on the novices that if they ever act otherwise, they will surely be condemned by the one they mock.

They state their promise in a document drawn up in the name of the saints whose relics are there and of the prioress or abbot, who is present. Novices write out this document themselves, or if they are illiterate, then they ask someone else to write it for them, but put their mark to it and with their own hand lay it on the altar. After they have put it there, the novice begins the verse: 'Receive me, O God, as you have promised, and I shall live; do not disappoint me in my hope' (Psalm 119:116). The whole community repeats the verse three times, and adds the Doxology. Then the novices prostrate themselves at the feet of each member to ask prayers, and from that very day they are to be counted as one of the community.

If they have any possessions, they should either give them to the poor beforehand, or make a formal donation of them to the monastery, without keeping back a single thing for themselves, well aware that from that day they will not have even their own body at their disposal. Then and there in the oratory, they are to be stripped of everything of their own that they are wearing and clothed in what belongs to the monastery. The clothing taken from them is to be put away and kept safely in the wardrobe, so that, should they ever agree to the devil's suggestion and leave the monastery – which God forbid – they can be stripped of the clothing of the monastery before they are cast out. But that document of theirs which the prioress or abbot took from the altar should not be given back to them but kept in the monastery.

Reflection

As we consider and respond to God's calling for each one of us, the principles of stability, conversion of life (change) and obedience (listening to God) become stronger and take on increased prominence. Stability and willingness to change are inextricably linked to listening to the voice of God.

Monks and nuns are required to surrender all their worldly goods. Maybe there are aspects of your life which you feel have to be surrendered to enable further stability, change and listening.

Write down your thoughts and ideas for enabling further stability, change and listening.

Read
Psalms 122–123

Pray
Receive me, O God, as you have promised, and I shall live; do not disappoint me in my hope.

13 Apr, 13 Aug, 13 Dec

Chapter 59: The offering of children by nobles or by the poor

If a member of the nobility offers a child to God in the monastery, and the child is too young, the parents draw up the document mentioned above; then, at the presentation of the gifts, they wrap the document itself and the child's hand in the altar cloth. That is how they make their offering.

As to their property, they either make a sworn promise in this document that they will never personally, never through an intermediary, nor in any way at all, nor at any time, give the child anything or afford the child the opportunity to possess anything; or else, if they are unwilling to do this and still wish to win their reward for making an offering to the monastery, they make a formal donation of the property that they want to give to the monastery, keeping the revenue for themselves, should they so desire. This ought to leave no way open for the child to entertain any expectations that could deceive and lead to ruin. May God forbid this, but we have learned from experience that it can happen.

Poor people do the same, but those who have nothing at all simply write the document and, in the presence of witnesses, offer their child with the gifts.

Reflection

In St Benedict's time, children were admitted to monastic communities. They came from rich and poor families but were allowed entry on exactly the same terms. As Joan Chittister observes, 'The poor have nothing whatsoever to give except their children and Benedict accepts them on the same grounds, with the same ceremony, in the same spirit. Benedictine spirituality does not fear poverty.'[72] Whatever one's background and upbringing, all are welcome in the kingdom of God.

In what ways does your church welcome children and people who are poor?

Read
Psalms 124—125

Pray
Help me to welcome and accept all the people I meet.

·····✝·····

14 Apr, 14 Aug, 14 Dec

Chapter 60: The admission of priests to the monastery

If any ordained priest asks to be received into a male monastery,[73] do not agree too quickly. However, if he is fully persistent in his request, he must recognize that he will have to observe the full discipline of the Rule without any mitigation, knowing that it is written: 'Friend, what have you come for?' (Matthew 26:50). He should, however, be allowed to stand next to the abbot, to give blessings and to celebrate the Eucharist, provided that the abbot bids him. Otherwise, he must recognize that he is subject to the discipline of the Rule, and not make any exceptions for himself, but rather give everyone an example of humility. Whenever there is question of an appointment or of any other business in the monastery, he takes the place that corresponds to the date of his entry into the community, and not that granted him out of respect for his priesthood.

Any clerics who similarly wish to join the community should be ranked somewhere in the middle, but only if they, too, promise to keep the Rule and observe stability.

Reflection

For many people, status is another fundamental contributor to stability. Whether that's in our job title or academic qualification, being a parent or a community stalwart, such matters influence our sense of identity. They are indicators of our importance in the eyes of others and of ourselves. Such 'status symbols' can be, as Norvene Vest describes them, like wanting 'a tidy little box that will give me a "code-word" I can use for others and myself to "verify" that I'm alright-with-God'. She also points out that labels (such as being ordained) describe functions not a relationship: 'The relationship may or may not coexist with the function [and the label] is no assurance of the relationship; often, in fact, it's a distraction from it.'[74]

Reflect on how your own 'status symbols' enhance and detract from your relationship with God.

Read
Psalms 126—127

Pray
Help me, Lord, simply to be the person you made me to be.

15 Apr, 15 Aug, 15 Dec

Chapter 61: The reception of visiting monastics

Visiting monastics from far away will perhaps present themselves and wish to stay as guests in the monastery. Provided that they are content with the life as they find it, and do not make excessive demands that upset the monastery, but are simply content with what they find, they should be received for as long a time as they wish. They may, indeed with all humility and love, make some reasonable criticisms or observations, which the prioress or abbot should prudently consider; it is possible that God guided them to the monastery for this very purpose.

If after a while they wish to remain and bind themselves to stability, they should not be refused this wish, especially as there was time enough, while they were a guest, to judge their character. But if during their stay they have been found excessive in their demands or full of faults, they should certainly not be admitted as a member of the community. Instead, they should be politely told to depart, lest their ways contaminate others.

Reflection

They say, 'Only fools rush in.'[75] We live in a world where politicians come into office and make immediate change, workplaces are constantly reorganised according to the chief executive's latest 'big idea' or the new minister alters the liturgy with no consultation. Whether business leader, politician or pastor – or none of those – we are but visitors: temporary residents with a duty of care for those with whom we reside.

This passage demonstrates the importance of acclimatising ourselves to situations and listening to the existing voices before expecting or making change – and then only doing so in humility and love. It's that word again – humility.

How do we seek to understand bigger pictures and respond to them wisely?

Read
Psalms 128—129

Pray
Help me to remember I am but a temporary resident.

16 Apr, 16 Aug, 16 Dec

Chapter 61: The reception of visiting monastics

If, however, they have shown that they are not the kind of persons who deserve to be dismissed, let them, on their request, be received as a member of the community. They should even be urged to stay, so that others may learn from their example, because wherever we may be, we are in the service of the same God. Further, the prioress or abbot may set such a person in a somewhat higher place in the community, if they see that they deserve it. The prioress or abbot has the power to set any one of them above the place that corresponds to the date of their entry, if they see that their life warrants it.

The prioress and abbot must, however, take care never to receive into the community anyone from another known monastery, unless the prioress or abbot of that community consents and sends a letter or recommendation, since it is written: 'Never do to another what you do not want done to yourself' (Tobit 4:15).

Reflection

Following on from yesterday's reading, having demonstrated humility and love and acknowledged that all are serving the same God and the same purposes, the newcomer may well be invited to share their gifts and, thinking back to chapter 60, to perhaps also use the benefits of their prior status.

As the apostle Peter put it, 'And all of you must clothe yourselves with humility in your dealings with one another, for "God opposes the proud, but gives grace to the humble." Humble yourselves therefore under the mighty hand of God, so that he may exalt you in due time' (1 Peter 5:5–6).

Think of a time when it was a humbling privilege to be asked to do something. What was it that made it special?

Read
Psalms 130—131

Pray
Thank you for the unexpected blessings and privileges you give us.

17 Apr, 17 Aug, 17 Dec

Chapter 62: The priests of the monastery

Any abbot of a male monastery who asks to have a priest or deacon ordained should choose from his monks one worthy to exercise the priesthood.[76] The monk so ordained must be on guard against conceit or pride, must not presume to do anything except what the abbot commands him, and must recognize that now he will have to subject himself all the more to the discipline of the Rule. Just because he is a priest, he may not therefore forget the obedience and discipline of the Rule, but must make more and more progress toward God.

He will always take the place that corresponds to the date of his entry into the monastery, except in his duties at the altar, or unless the whole community chooses and the abbot wishes to give him a higher place for the goodness of his life. Yet, he must know how to keep the Rule established for deans and priors; should he presume to act otherwise, he must be regarded as a rebel, not as a priest. If after many warnings he does not improve, let the bishop too be brought in as a witness. Should he not amend even then, and his faults become notorious, he is to be dismissed from the monastery, but only if he is so arrogant that he will not submit or obey the Rule.

Reflection

Vocation is something to which we are called by God – it carries no hierarchy. We are not set on different levels, only different paths. As well as ordination, God calls to secular occupation, the bringing-up of children, caring for others, voluntary work and numerous other ways of fulfilling and using the gifts that he has given. Occasionally, such calling may be crystal clear; other times, we may not realise we've found our vocation until after it's begun.

God calls us and gives us a choice to accept, ignore or refuse that calling. God calls us and enables us to make more and more progress towards him.

Do have a sense of your vocation? In what ways do you sense God is calling you to make more and more progress towards him?

Read
Psalm 132

Pray
I am your servant, Lord, and I long to hear your calling.

18 Apr, 18 Aug, 18 Dec

Chapter 63: Community rank

Monastics keep their rank in the monastery according to the date of their entry, the virtue of their lives, and the decision of the prioress or abbot. The prioress or abbot is not to disturb the flock entrusted to them nor make any unjust arrangements, as though they had the power to do whatever they wished. They must constantly reflect that they will have to give God an account of all their decisions and actions. Therefore, when the members come for the kiss of peace and for Communion, when they lead Psalms or stand in choir, they do so in the order already existing among them or decided by the abbot or prioress. Absolutely nowhere shall age automatically determine rank. Remember that Samuel and Daniel were still boys when they judged their elders (1 Samuel 3; Daniel 13:44–62). Therefore, apart from those mentioned above whom the abbot or prioress have for some overriding consideration promoted, or for a specific reason demoted, all the rest should keep to the order of their entry. For example, someone who came to the monastery at the second hour of the day must recognize that they are junior to someone who came at the first hour, regardless of age or distinction. The young, however, are to be disciplined in everything by everyone.

Reflection

When we were younger, we didn't understand what it was really like to be older. When we are old, we may forget what it was like to be young.

The dynamics of age and long-standing presence can be very complex. It is common for older, experienced workers to find having a much younger manager to be very difficult. Then again, younger people coming into positions of leadership can feel 'looked down' upon because of age and lack of experience. And then we have longer-standing 'inhabitants' of a position or role who may assume or are treated with some kind of preferential status and power.

Reflect on a time when age proved a barrier or was an enhancement to a relationship with someone else.

Read
Psalms 133—134

Pray
May I see all people for who they are, regardless of age.

·····†·····

19 Apr, 19 Aug, 19 Dec

Chapter 63: Community rank

The younger monastics, then, must respect their elders, and the elders must love their juniors. When they address one another, no one should be allowed to do so simply by name: rather, the elders call the younger 'sister' or 'brother' and the younger members call their elders 'nonna' or 'nonnus' which is translated as 'venerable one.' But the abbot and prioress, because we believe that they hold the place of Christ, are to be called 'abbot' or 'prioress' not for any claim of their own, but out of honour and love for Christ. They for their part, must reflect on this and in their behaviour show themselves worthy of such honour.

Wherever members meet, the junior asks the elder for a blessing. When older members come by, the younger ones rise and offers them a seat, and do not presume to sit down unless the older bids them. In this way, they do what the words of scripture say: 'They should each try to be the first to show respect for the other' (Romans 12:10).

In the oratory and at table, the young are kept in rank and under discipline. Outside or anywhere else, they should be supervised and controlled until they are old enough to be responsible.

Reflection

Respect works both ways. Younger people are to respect the experience, wisdom and knowledge of their elders. Older people are to respect those who are younger and enable them to flourish and grow. Both can learn from each other. Each person, regardless of age, is unique.

But there is also a deeper message here about how these relationships between individuals, young or old, are conducted with honour and love for Christ. '[Benedict] is giving us a basis for right relationships,' writes Esther de Waal, 'the working out of an interdependence and complementarity of one with another which can link us all into a mysterious, unseen communion with each other in and through the figure of Christ himself.'[77]

Looking back over your life so far:
● What have you learnt from younger people?
● What have you learnt from older people?

Read
Psalm 135

Pray
Help me to value the experience and wisdom of everyone, regardless of age.

20 Apr, 20 Aug, 20 Dec

Chapter 64: The election of a prioress or abbot

In choosing an abbot or prioress, the guiding principle should always be that the one placed in office be the one selected either by the whole community acting unanimously out of reverence for God, or by some part of the community no matter how small, which possesses sounder judgment. Goodness of life and wisdom in teaching must be the criteria for choosing the one to be made abbot or prioress even if they are the last in community rank.

May God forbid that a whole community should conspire to elect a prioress or abbot who goes along with its own evil ways. But if it does, and if the bishop of the diocese or any Benedictine leaders or other Christians in the area come to know of these evil ways to any extent, they must block the success of this wicked conspiracy, and set a worthy person in charge of God's house. They may be sure that they will receive a generous reward for this, if they do it with pure motives and zeal for God's honour. Conversely, they may be equally sure that to neglect to do so is sinful.

Reflection

The early chapters of the *Rule* considered the qualities of leadership, and now, as we gradually approach the end, St Benedict revisits this important topic. Many a government, workplace and religious organisation has been torn apart by poor appointments or political manoeuvring where personal ambition rose above the needs and aims of a wider community. We probably all know victims and perpetrators of such – perhaps there have been times when you have been one.

St Benedict's message remains clear: our leaders are to be people who demonstrate goodness of life and wise teaching. They are to work with pure motives and a passion, a zeal, for God's honour. Sometimes such high standards will come into conflict with the contrary ideals and persuasions of others, and it is difficult for leaders to lead if the community is not behind them.

Think back on your time with the *Rule* and how has it affected your support for the leaders you know.

Read
Psalm 136

Pray
Thank you for the people I know who are in leadership positions.

·····✝·····

21 Apr, 21 Aug, 21 Dec

Chapter 64: The election of a prioress or abbot

Once in office, the abbot and prioress must keep constantly in mind the nature of the burden they have received, and remember to whom they will have 'to give an account of their stewardship' (Luke 16:2). Let them recognize that the goal must be profit for the community members, not pre-eminence for themselves. They ought, therefore, to be learned in divine law, so that they have a treasury of knowledge from which they can 'bring out what is new and what is old' (Matthew 13:52). The abbot and prioress must be chaste, temperate and merciful, always letting 'mercy triumph over judgment' (James 2:13) so that they too may win mercy. They must hate faults but love the members. When they must punish them, they should use prudence and avoid extremes; otherwise, by rubbing too hard to remove the rust, they may break the vessel. They are to distrust their own frailty and remember 'not to crush the bruised reed' (Isaiah 42:3). By this we do not mean that they should allow faults to flourish, but rather, as we have already said, they should prune them away with prudence and love as they see best for each individual. Let them strive to be loved rather than feared.

Excitable, anxious, extreme, obstinate, jealous or overly suspicious the abbot or prioress must not be. Such a person is never at rest. Instead, they must show forethought and consideration in their orders and whether the task they assign concerns God or the world, they should be discerning and moderate, bearing in mind the discretion of holy Jacob, who said: 'If I drive my flocks too hard, they will all die in a single day' (Genesis 33:13). Therefore, drawing on this and other examples of discretion, they must so arrange everything that the strong have something to yearn for and the weak nothing to run from.

They must, above all, keep this Rule in every detail, so that when they have ministered well they will hear from God what that good servant heard who gave the other members of the household grain at the proper time: 'I tell you solemnly, God will put this one in charge of greater things' (Matthew 24:47).

Reflection

In chapter 4, we were given a toolbox for good works. Here, St Benedict offers a toolbox for good leadership:

- Always able to take responsibility for decisions.
- Always aiming for the best for others and the common goals – not pre-eminence for themselves.

- Able to draw on their knowledge and experience.
- To be even-tempered and fair.
- To deal with mistakes carefully and maintain love for those who make them.
- To strive to be loved, not feared.
- To be calm, reasoned and trustworthy.
- To delegate tasks to the right person.
- To encourage those with less confidence.

Read
Psalms 137—138

Pray
Help our leaders to use their position well.

·····†·····

22 Apr, 22 Aug, 22 Dec

Chapter 65: The prior and subprioress of the monastery

Too often in the past, the appointment of a subprioress or prior has been the source of serious contention in monasteries. Some, puffed up by the evil spirit of pride and thinking of themselves as a second prioress or abbot, usurp tyrannical power and foster contention and discord in their communities. This occurs especially in monasteries where the same bishop and the same prioress or abbot appoint both the abbot and prioress and the prior or subprioress. It is easy to see what an absurd arrangement this is, because from the very first moment of appointment they are given grounds for pride, as their thoughts suggest to them that they are exempt from the authority of the prioress or abbot. 'After all, you were made subprioress or prior by the same members who made the prioress or abbot.'

This is an open invitation to envy, quarrels, slander, rivalry, factions and disorders of every kind, with the result that, while the prioress and subprioress or abbot and prior pursue conflicting policies, their own souls are inevitably endangered by this discord; and at the same time the monastics under them take sides and so go to their ruin. The responsibility for this evil and dangerous situation rests on the heads of those who initiated such a state of confusion.

Reflection

While perhaps written from a point of personal frustration and despair at the time, St Benedict's observations of human nature remain as relevant today as they were then. 'Benedict is completely realistic about human nature and its weaknesses and not least what happens when pride sets in,' writes Esther de Waal. 'We can see it at work in a marriage... and damage the whole family; in a parish where people split into factions and tear the congregation apart; in a community caught up in a power struggle and living off negative energy because it fails to deal with the underlying issues.'[78]

Spend time praying for a situation you know about.

Read
Psalm 139

Pray
'Search me, O God, and know my heart; test me and know my thoughts' (Psalm 139:23).

·····✝·····

23 Apr, 23 Aug, 23 Dec

Chapter 65: The prior and subprioress of the monastery

For the preservation of peace and love we have, therefore, judged it best for the abbot or prioress to make all decisions in the conduct of the monastery. If possible, as we have already established, the whole operation of the monastery should be managed through deans under the directions of the abbot or prioress. Then, so long as it is entrusted to more than one, no individual will yield to pride. But if local conditions call for it, or the community makes a reasonable and humble request, and the prioress or abbot judges it best, then let them, with the advice of members who reverence God, choose the one they want and themselves make that one the subprioress or prior. The subprioress and prior for their part are to carry out respectfully what the prioress or abbot assigns, and do nothing contrary to their wishes or arrangements, because the more they are set above the rest, the more they should be concerned to keep what the Rule commands.

If these subprioresses or priors are found to have serious faults, or are led astray by conceit and grow proud, or show open contempt for the holy Rule, they are to be warned verbally as many as four times. If they do not amend, they are to be punished as required by the discipline of the Rule. Then, if they still do not reform they are to be deposed from the rank of subprioress or prior and replaced by someone worthy. If after all that, they are not peaceful and obedient members of the community, they should even be expelled from the monastery. Yet the abbot or prioress should reflect that they must give God an account of all their judgments, lest the flames of jealousy or rivalry sear their soul.

Reflection

When such situations occur as those we reflected on yesterday, it can take a long time to heal the hurt that has been caused. Such situations need people with particular skills who can work with others to preserve peace and love and reduce the pride which has caused so much damage. 'If Benedict knows how destructive divergent and centrifugal elements can be,' writes Esther de Waal, 'he also knows the importance of accepting the wide range and variety of human nature and human experience. The question is how to hold these elements together and so integrate them that the whole body becomes life-giving rather than life-denying.'[79]

Return to thinking about the situation you prayed about yesterday. Ask God to further your insight into the way forward.

Read
Psalms 140—141

Pray
'I call upon you, O Lord; come quickly to me; give ear to my voice when I call to you' (Psalm 141:1).

24 Apr, 24 Aug, 24 Dec

Chapter 66: The porter of the monastery

At the door of the monastery, place a sensible person who knows how to take a message and deliver a reply, and whose wisdom keeps them from roaming about. This porter will need a room near the entrance so that visitors will always find someone there to answer them. As soon as anyone knocks, or a poor person calls out, the porter will reply, 'Thanks be to God' or 'Your blessing, please', then, with all the gentleness that comes from reverence of God, provides a prompt answer with the warmth of love. Let the porter be given one of the younger members if help is needed.

The monastery should, if possible, be so constructed that within it all necessities, such as water, mill and garden are contained, and the various crafts are practiced. Then there will be no need for the members to roam outside, because this is not at all good for their souls.

We wish this Rule to be read often in the community, so that none of the members can offer the excuse of ignorance.

Reflection

How we are welcomed somewhere has such an impact on us, doesn't it? You've arrived at a hotel or an appointment… and there's no one on reception. Or you've visited a church where the lack of welcome speaks volumes. Such things not only make us feel unwelcome but can temporarily affect our stability.

Contrast that with the delight and reassurance of a warm welcome. If the welcome is good, we are more likely to feel at home and to want to return. And if we feel welcomed as if we are Christ, as the *Rule* exhorts, then we will have been greeted with all the love and gentleness that comes from God. What a welcome that would be!

Think back to chapter 53. What are you now seeing of Christ in the people you meet?

Read
Psalms 142—143

Pray
May I look for Christ in all people.

·····†·····

25 Apr, 25 Aug, 25 Dec

Chapter 67: Members sent on a journey

Members sent on a journey will ask the prioress or abbot and the community to pray for them. All absent members should always be remembered at the closing prayer of the Opus Dei. When they come back from a journey, they should, on the very day of their return, lie face down on the floor of the oratory at the conclusion of each of the customary hours of the Opus Dei. They ask the prayers of all for their faults, in case they may have been caught off guard on the way by seeing some evil thing or hearing some idle talk.

No monastics should presume to relate to anyone else what they saw or heard outside the monastery, because that causes the greatest harm. If any do so presume, they shall be subjected to the punishment of the Rule. So too shall anyone who presumes to leave the enclosure of the monastery, or go anywhere, or do anything at all, however small, without the order of the abbot or the prioress.

Reflection

When travelling from a place of safety to other, perhaps unfamiliar, surroundings, it is so good to know that other people are praying for us. Unlike in the time of the *Rule*, where the knowledge of the outside world was viewed as having a bad influence on fellow monastics, it is good for us to be able to share what we saw and learned, what we talked about, who we met and, maybe, what went wrong.

In December, this reading falls on Christmas Day. Reflect on the journeys taken by Joseph and Mary and by the shepherds. What would they be talking about?

In April, think back to Easter and those who witnessed the crucifixion or the resurrection. What contrasting stories might they be telling?

In August, we can think of holidays: the joys and the tensions they can bring. Try writing a postcard to yourself about your experience of God in such times.

Read
Psalm 144

Pray
Pray for those you know to be taking a journey today.

26 Apr, 26 Aug, 26 Dec

Chapter 68: Assignment of impossible tasks

Monastics may be assigned a burdensome task or something they cannot do. If so, they should, with complete gentleness and obedience, accept the order given them. Should they see, however, that the weight of the burden is altogether too much for their strength, then they should choose the appropriate moment and explain patiently to the prioress or abbot the reasons why they cannot perform the task. This they ought to do without pride, obstinacy or refusal. If after the explanation the abbot or prioress is still determined to hold to their original order, then the junior must recognize that this is best. Trusting in God's help, they must in love obey.

Reflection

Whether it's at work, church or home, we can be faced with seemingly impossible tasks. Our natural response may be 'I ought to be able to do this' or 'I should be able to cope'. But these 'oughts' and 'shoulds' are not always helpful. And yet we can be reluctant to ask for help.

Asking for help, though, is a great strength and not a sign of weakness or failure. Asking for help is not only an open acknowledgement of something we need but is an active fulfilment of the Bible's teachings to 'bear one another's burdens' (Galatians 6:2). Other people will say to us, 'Let me know If I can do anything to help.' Yet how often do we actually take up that offer? We don't like to bother people. We think they've got enough on their plate without our adding to that. Yet accepting such offers of help not only eases the burdens we carry but it also affirms the ones who offer and provide assistance and, just as importantly, it builds up community and glorifies God.

Is there someone whose offer of help could be accepted? Do you need to ask for help?

Read
Psalm 145

Pray
May I learn how to serve and to be served.

······ † ······

27 Apr, 27 Aug, 27 Dec

Chapter 69: The presumption of defending another in the monastery

Every precaution must be taken that one member does not presume in any circumstance to defend another in the monastery or to be their champion, even if they are related by the closest ties of blood. In no way whatsoever shall monastics presume to do this, because it can be a most serious source and occasion of contention. Anyone who breaks this rule is to be sharply restrained.

Reflection

Esther de Waal writes: 'When I fail to face what has to be faced, or to grasp what has to be grasped, but instead try to find people who will support me (probably finding those who will listen to my story and encourage me to think that my cause is right), I have succumbed to a very pernicious way of dealing with my problem. Before long I may well begin to see my world as divided into factions, those who believe my story and those who do not.'[80]

We learn to 'take sides' at a very early age. We stick by people against others. We champion particular causes. We manipulate other people to agree with our point of view – even when we are in the wrong. Such approaches, while very natural and sometimes justifiable, create tension and conflict with others.

In what ways might you fall into such situations?

Read
Psalm 146

Pray
Please forgive me when I manipulate others.

·····†·····

28 Apr, 28 Aug, 28 Dec

Chapter 70: The presumption of striking another monastic at will

In the monastery every occasion for presumption is to be avoided, and so we decree that no one has the authority to excommunicate or strike any member of the community unless given this power by the prioress or abbot. 'Those who sin should be reprimanded in the presence of all, that the rest may fear' (1 Timothy 5:20). The young up to the age of fifteen should, however, be carefully controlled and supervised by everyone, provided that this too is done with moderation and common sense.

If any member, without the command of the abbot or prioress, assumes any power over those older or, even in regard to the young, flares up and treats them unreasonably, let that one be subjected to the discipline of the Rule. After all, it is written: 'Never do to another what you do not want done to yourself' (Tobit 4:15).

Reflection

Continuing yesterday's theme, these are difficult words for our modern eyes but, as Joan Chittister explains, 'Benedictine spirituality depended on personal commitment and community support, not on intimidation and brutality. Benedict makes it clear that the desire for good is no excuse for the exercise of evil in its behalf. This is an important chapter, then, for people whose high ideals lead them to the basest of means in the name of the achievement of good.'[81]

We are to be aware of abusing power or assuming authority when it is not ours to have.

More self-examination is necessary: how might this resonate with you?

Read
Psalm 147

Pray
Please help me to be pure in motive.

·····✝·····

29 Apr, 29 Aug, 29 Dec

Chapter 71: Mutual obedience

Obedience is a blessing to be shown by all, not only to the prioress and abbot but also to one another, since we know that it is by this way of obedience that we go to God. Therefore, although orders of the prioress and abbot or of the subprioress or prior appointed by them take precedence, and no unofficial order may supersede them, in every other instance younger members should obey their elders with all love and concern. Anyone found objecting to this should be reproved.

If a member is reproved in any way by the abbot or prioress or by one of the elders, even for some very small matter, or gets the impression that one of the elders is angry or disturbed with them, however slightly, that member must, then and there without delay, fall down on the ground at the other's feet to make satisfaction, and lie there until the disturbance is calmed by a blessing. Anyone who refuses to do this should be subjected to corporal punishment or, if stubborn, should be expelled from the monastery.

Reflection

Of the many themes that run through the *Rule*, obedience and the resolution of conflict are two particularly important ones – and listening is fundamental to both of them. Whoever we might be and in whatever situation we find ourselves, listening is an integral element in the fulfilment and expression of our love for one another and for God. The absence of listening quickly creates conflict. It is therefore imperative that listening is reinstated as soon as possible so as to achieve understanding and seek resolution: 'There is no question here of who is in the right or of what might have prompted the behaviour that has caused the upset,' writes David Foster. 'The precept is about taking the initiative in making a different future possible.'[82]

These last three chapters have explored uncomfortable realities of human existence. Reflect on what you have considered and learnt.

Read
Psalm 148

Pray
May I seek to make a different future possible.

·····†·····

30 Apr, 30 Aug, 30 Dec

Chapter 72: The good zeal of monastics

> Just as there is a wicked zeal of bitterness which separates from God and leads to hell, so there is a good zeal which separates from evil and leads to God and everlasting life. This, then, is the good zeal which members must foster with fervent love: 'They should each try to be the first to show respect to the other' (Romans 12:10), supporting with the greatest patience one another's weaknesses of body or behaviour, and earnestly competing in obedience to one another. No monastics are to pursue what they judge better for themselves, but instead, what they judge better for someone else. Among themselves they show the pure love of sisters and brothers; to God, reverent love; to their prioress or abbot, unfeigned and humble love. Let them prefer nothing

whatever to Christ, and may Christ bring us all together to everlasting life.

Reflection

'Our faith is not in a cause, a campaign, a church,' said Timothy Bavin. 'Our faith is in a personal God, and we are to prefer nothing whatever to Christ.'[83]

In chapter 43, the *Rule* advocated that 'nothing is to be preferred to the Opus Dei'. Here, we are exhorted to 'prefer nothing whatever to Christ'. The Opus Dei, the Work of God, is the outworking of our wholehearted devotion to Christ himself.

A tall order? Yes.

One we will achieve? No, not in this earthly lifetime. But as the *Rule* has taught us, if we set out with humility, reverence, obedience, a willingness to change and a love for our fellow beings, we will go some way to being together in Christ.

Read
Psalm 149

Pray
'Take my life, and let it be consecrated, Lord to thee.'[84]

1 May, 31 Aug, 31 Dec

Chapter 73: This Rule is only a beginning of perfection

The reason we have written this Rule is that, by observing it in monasteries, we can show that we have some degree of virtue and the beginnings of monastic life. But for anyone hastening on to the perfection of monastic life, there are the teachings of the early church writers, the observance of which will lead them to the very heights of perfection. What page, what passage of the inspired books of the Old and New Testaments is not the truest of guides for human life? What book of holy writers does not resoundingly summon us along the true way to reach the Creator? Then, besides the Conferences[85] of the early church writers, their Institutes[86] and their Lives,[87] there is also the Rule of Basil.[88] For observant and obedient monastics, all these are nothing less than tools for the cultivation of virtues; but as for us, they make us blush for shame at being so slothful, so unobservant, so negligent. Are you hastening toward your heavenly home? Then with Christ's help, keep this little Rule that we have written for beginners. After that, you can set out for the loftier summits of the teaching and virtues we mentioned above, and under God's protection you will reach them. Amen.

Reflection

While we have come to the end of the *Rule of St Benedict*, in many respects we are all beginners. Everything we know about God is simply the equivalent of the first stroke of a pen. From the days of the Bible, through the teachers and writers of the early church, right up to modern day theologians and preachers, the wisdom of centuries has fashioned tools for daily living: tools which not only cultivate virtue but also hasten us towards our heavenly home. There is so much more to come.

As we live out our faith, we come to listen more. As we listen, we find stability and we meet a God who changes us; a God who makes us into the person he wants us to be; a God who draws us ever closer towards our heavenly home.

Looking back over the past four months, in what ways have you:

- Learnt to listen more and obey God?
- Found increased stability?
- Changed?

Read
Psalm 150

Pray
Thank you, Lord, for all I have learned. May my beginning be never-ending. Amen

I think that maybe
I will be a little surer
of being a little nearer.
That's all. Eternity
is in the understanding
that that little is more than enough.

'Eternity is More Than Enough' by R.S. Thomas[89]

A Rule of Life

Women and men undertaking a commitment to be an oblate to a Benedictine community have a written personal Rule of Life that reflects their individual circumstances. By this Rule of Life, the oblate witnesses to the gospel through their relationship with those among whom they live and work. That said, in many respects, anyone can have a Rule of Life and while the example that follows is loosely based on that used by oblates at the Anglican Benedictine Community at Alton Abbey in Hampshire and includes some suggested basic commitments, it is quite possible to individually tailor it to suit and take into account your personal situation.

1 To conform his or her life to the spirit of the *Rule of St Benedict*.

2 Daily to pray a specified portion of the Divine Office.

3 To practise regular and frequent attendance at church, especially for Holy Communion.

4 To practise regular prayer, both formal and meditative.

5 To make time for spiritual reading (e.g. *lectio divina*).

6 To make an annual retreat.

7 To use confession and spiritual direction as often as may be appropriate.

8 To make the life and work of a Benedictine community a regular intention of prayer.

9 To practise regular almsgiving.

10 To make adequate provision for study, recreation and the needs of family commitment and personal relationship.

You may like to copy out those headings and then write some further comments about what you will do. But keep it realistic. God wants you to be who you are, not someone you are not.

More information about becoming an oblate can be found at **benedictine-oblates.net**.

Some monastic communities are gender- and/or denomination-specific, so do contact them directly.

Further reading

Ampleforth Abbey, *The Benedictine Handbook*
(Canterbury Press, 2003)

Joan Chittister OSB, *The Rule of Benedict*
(Crossroad Publishing, 1992)

Eric Dean, *Saint Benedict for the Laity* (The Liturgical Press, 1989)

David Foster OSB, *Deep Calls to Deep* (Bloomsbury, 2012)

Thelma Hall r.c., *Too Deep for Words* (Paulist Press, 1988)

Gervase Holdaway (ed.), *The Oblate Life*
(OSB Canterbury Press, 2008)

Abbot Christopher Jamison, *Finding Sanctuary*
(Weidenfeld & Nicholson, 2006)

Barbara Brown Taylor, *When God is Silent* (Canterbury Press, 2013)

Ambrose Tinsley OSB, *Carried by the Current* (Columba Press, 2004)

Jane Tomaine, *St Benedict's Toolbox: The nuts and bolts of everyday
Benedictine living* (Morehouse Publishing, 2015)

Norvene Vest, *Preferring Christ* (Morehouse Publishing, 1990)

Esther de Waal, *A Life-Giving Way* (Canterbury Press, 2013)

Esther de Waal, *Seeking God* (Canterbury Press, 1999)

Notes

1 Sculpture © Sister Concordia Scott OSB. Photograph © Richard Frost.

2 Richard Moth, talk at Oblate Retreat, Douai Abbey, 2008, **benedictine-oblates.net/wp-content/uploads/2017/04/douaitalk3. doc**.

3 Pope Francis, 'Obedience is a listening that sets us free', April 2013, **osservatoreromano.va/en/news/obedience-is-a-listening-that-sets-us-free**.

4 The numbering of psalms and the verses within them vary according to whether the Hebrew (Masoretic) or the Greek (Septuagint) text is used. In this book, the Hebrew numbering system is adopted as used in the New Revised Standard Version (NRSV). There may be occasional differences from the numbering used in other versions of the Bible.

5 *A Reader's Version of the Rule of Saint Benedict* in Inclusive Language © Benedictine Sisters of Erie, 1989 (updated at **eriebenedictines. org/daily-rule**). Used by kind permission. This version is adapted from RB 1980 © 1981 The Order of Saint Benedict Inc, Collegeville, Minnesota, edited by Timothy Fry OSB.

6 Biblical chapter and verse references throughout this book are as used in the NRSV. The text from verses quoted in the extracts from the *Rule* is as used in *A Reader's Version of the Rule of Saint Benedict*.

7 *Book of Common Prayer* (1662), orders for morning and evening prayer.

8 Rowan Williams, *Being Christian* (SPCK, 2014), p. 65.

9 No definitive accreditation is known.

10 David Foster OSB, *Deep Calls to Deep* (Bloomsbury, 2012), p. 123.

11 Giles Hill OSB, author's notes from a talk at Oblates' Retreat, Alton Abbey, 2016.

12 Joan Chittister OSB, *The Rule of Benedict* (Crossroad Publishing, 1992), p. 29.

13 Rotha Mary Clay, *Hermits and Anchorites of England*, quoted in 'How I became a medieval-style anchorite', *Catholic Herald*, 29 February

2012, **catholicherald.co.uk/news/2012/02/29/how-i-became-a-medieval-style-anchorite**, 2012.

14 Janet Arthur, 'Leadership defined', *The Connexion 9* (Autumn, 2017), pp. 18–19.

15 Sirach, also known as Ecclesiasticus or Book of the All-Virtuous Wisdom of Joshua ben Sira, is one of the books of the Apocrypha.

16 *Lectio divina* is not Bible study; it is about pondering on the word to enable prayer. Stages comprise reading just a verse or a short passage two or three times (*lectio*); then meditation, taking a word or phrase and ruminating upon it (*meditatio*); leading into prayer: open, honest conversation with God (*oratio*); and then resting in God, the silent prayer of contemplation (*contemplatio*).

17 Brother Lawrence, *The Practice of the Presence of God* (Mockingbird Classics Publishing, 2015), p. 55.

18 Attributed to Jean-Baptiste Alphonse Karr, French critic, journalist and novelist (1808–90).

19 Chittister, *The Rule of Benedict*, p. 60.

20 John Baldoni, *Lead by Example* (Marshall Goldsmith, 2008).

21 Esther de Waal, *Seeking God* (Canterbury Press, 1999), p. 136.

22 See note 15.

23 Oprah Winfrey, commencement address at Johnson C. Smith University in North Carolina, 2016, **news.harvard.edu/gazette/story/2013/05/winfreys-commencement-address**.

24 Saint Anastasia of Sirmium (died AD304).

25 Peter Funk OSB, 'Becoming a different kind of person', 28 July 2015, **chicagomonk.org/about-us/the-priors-blog/becoming-a-different-kind-of-person**.

26 Foster, *Deep Calls to Deep*, p. 128.

27 Philip Lawrence OSB, 'Chapter 7: Humility', **christdesert.org/prayer/rule-of-st-benedict/chapter-7-humility**.

28 Oscar Wilde, *The Picture of Dorian Gray* (Penguin Classics, 2000, 2003).

29 The Sentences of Sextus, *Enchiridion*, 134 or 145.

30 Barbara Brown Taylor, *When God is Silent* (Canterbury Press, 2013), pp. 99, 113.

31 Chittister, *The Rule of Benedict*, p. 74.

32 Esther de Waal, *A Life-Giving Way* (Canterbury Press, 2013), p. 161.

33 An explanation of the structure of Divine Office, as it is also called, can be found in the glossary on page 14.

34 Michael Perham, 'St Benedict and Anglican worship', an address at

the Annual Meeting of the Alcuin Club, 2006.

35 Often referred to as 'patristic', daily patterns of such readings can be found in variety of books (e.g. a breviary) and online (e.g. **readthefathers.org**).

36 An alternative name for the book of Revelation.

37 Based on the Prayer of Azariah verses 29–68 in the Apocrypha, also known as Benedicite and used in Anglican liturgy. Abednego was originally called Azariah (Daniel 1:6–7).

38 Nadia Bolz-Weber, from the author's notes of a talk given at Festival of Preaching, Oxford, 2017.

39 The Second Song of Moses (Deuteronomy 32:1–43).

40 Ambrose Tinsley OSB, *Carried by the Current* (Columba Press, 2004), p. 44.

41 Author unknown, 'Early monastic office', **christdesert.org/prayer/ opus-dei/early-monastic-office**.

42 Perham, 'St Benedict and Anglican worship'.

43 de Waal, *Seeking God*, p. 132.

44 Tinsley, *Carried by the Current*, p. 47.

45 Foster, *Deep Calls to Deep*, pp. 9–10.

46 Excommunication has been described as a 'medicinal penalty' intended to invite the person to change the behaviour or attitude that incurred the penalty, to repent and to return to full communion (Roman Catholic *Code of Canon Law*, Can. 1,312:, **vatican.va/archive/ ENG1104/__P4U.HTM**).

47 Chittister, *The Rule of Benedict*, p. 104.

48 Augustine of Hippo, 'Sermons, Mai 14.1–2', *Patrologiae Latinae Supplementum*, 2.449–450, edited by A. Hamman; quoted in Mark Holmes, *Celebrating Sundays* (Canterbury Press, 2012), p. 257.

49 **trusselltrust.org/news-and-blog/latest-stats**.

50 **equalityhumanrights.com/en/secondary-education-resources/ useful-information/understanding-equality**.

51 Most translations locate this in The Prayer of Azariah, verse 29 (see also note 37).

52 Jada Pryor, 'Top 7 Bible verses about old age or the elderly', **patheos. com/blogs/christiancrier/2015/06/24/top-7-bible-verses-about- old-age-or-the-elderly/#0SHEybi50MilVmC6.99**, 2015.

53 David Winter, *The Highway Code for Retirement* (CWR, 2012), p. 8.

54 In St Benedict's time, this was called a *hemina* and is equivalent to 0.75 litre: the modern equivalent of five units a day. Today, in the UK, 14 units per week is the recommended limit.

55   Norvene Vest, *Preferring Christ* (Morehouse Publishing, 1990),
     pp. 173–74.

56   A reference to *Conferences of the Desert Fathers* by John Cassian
     (c. 360–435).

57   A reference to the *Vitae Patrum (Lives of the Fathers)*, a collection
     of writings of the Desert Fathers and Desert Mothers of early
     Christianity, most of which date from the third and fourth century.

58   The first seven books of the Hebrew Bible: Genesis, Exodus,
     Leviticus, Numbers, Deuteronomy, Joshua and Judges.

59   de Waal, *A Life-Giving Way*, p. 130.

60   From 'Dear Lord and Father of mankind' by John Greenleaf Whittier
     (1807–92).

61   Brown Taylor, *When God is Silent*, pp. 121, 118.

62   Timothy Bavin OSB, from the author's notes from Oblates' Retreat,
     Alton Abbey, 2017.

63   de Waal, *A Life-Giving Way*, p. 133.

64   Michael Cowan, 'Superheroes don't work 90-hour weeks', 17 January
     2018, **bbc.co.uk/news/business-42705291**.

65   Gordon Waddell and A. Kim Burton, *Is Work Good for Your Health and
     Wellbeing?* (The Stationery Office, 2008).

66   *Five Ways to Wellbeing* was produced by the New Economics
     Foundation on behalf of Foresight 2008. For more information, visit
     gov.uk/government/publications/five-ways-to-mental-wellbeing.

67   Thomas Kardong OSB, *Conversation with Saint Benedict* (Liturgical
     Press, 2012), p. 6.

68   Chittister, *The Rule of Benedict*, p. 138.

69   de Waal, *Seeking God*, p. 105.

70   Chittister, *The Rule of Benedict*, p. 148.

71   Bavin, from the author's notes from Oblates' Retreat, Alton Abbey,
     2017.

72   Chittister, *The Rule of Benedict*, p. 156.

73   For the purposes of this book, the principles of this chapter should
     be assumed to apply equally to a woman priest seeking admission to
     a female community, as appropriate to the denomination.

74   Vest, *Preferring Christ*, p. 232.

75   From Alexander Pope's 'Essay on Criticism' (1709).

76   See note 73.

77   de Waal, *A Life-Giving Way*, p. 191.

78   de Waal, *A Life-Giving Way*, pp. 198–99.

79   de Waal, *A Life-Giving Way*, p. 199.

80 de Waal, *A Life-Giving Way*, p. 206.

81 Chittister, *The Rule of Benedict*, p. 175.

82 Foster, *Deep Calls to Deep*, p. 127.

83 Bavin, from the author's notes from Oblates' Retreat, Alton Abbey, 2017.

84 'Take my life' by Frances Ridley Havergal (1836–79).

85 See note 56.

86 A reference to *Institutes of the Coenobia* by John Cassian (c. 360–435). Coenobia are monastic communities with a focus on communal life and not solitude or seclusion from society – as in cenobites (see chapter 1).

87 See note 57.

88 A reference to *The Rule of Basil* by Basil the Great, bishop of Caesarea (c. 330–379).

89 R.S. Thomas, 'Eternity is More Than Enough' in *Collected Later Poems 1988–2000* (Bloodaxe Books, 2004). Reproduced with permission of Bloodaxe Books. **www.bloodaxebooks.com**.

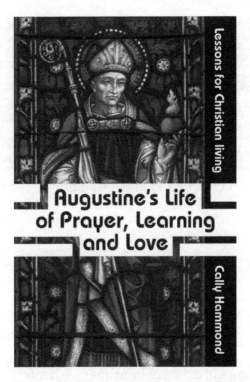

There are many books that tell the life story of Augustine and how he has been fundamental in shaping western Christian theology and practice. This is not one of them. This book is about how he became a Christian – the problems he faced; the doubts he struggled with. It is about how he made sense of his belief in God, and shared it with other people. It is about how he learned to read the Bible, and to pray. And it is about the word which is at the heart of his Christian life – love. It concludes with moments of prayer from Augustine's life, in which he glimpses visions of God, encouraging the reader to take their own next steps in discipleship.

Augustine's Life of Prayer, Learning and Love
Lessons for Christian living
Cally Hammond
978 0 85746 713 3 £8.99

brfonline.org.uk

BRF

Transforming
lives and communities

Christian growth and understanding of the Bible

Resourcing individuals, groups and leaders in churches for their
own spiritual journey and for their ministry

Church outreach in the local community

Offering two programmes that churches
are embracing to great effect as they
seek to engage with their local
communities and transform lives

Teaching Christianity in primary schools

Working with children and teachers to explore Christianity
creatively and confidently

Children's and family ministry

Working with churches and families to explore
Christianity creatively and bring the Bible alive

parenting for faith

Visit **brf.org.uk** for more information on BRF's work

brf.org.uk